NuWave Oven Heavenly Cookbook
Fast Delicious Recipes For Very Busy People

Angelica B. Anderson

NMD Books
Simi Valley, CA

Library of Congress Cataloging-in-Publication

NuWave Oven Heavenly Cookbook:
Fast Delicious Recipes For Very Busy People
by Angelica B. Anderson

ISBN: 978-1-936828-32-6

First Edition January 2015

Contents

Introduction

Perhaps the most sought after feature of an oven today is the ability to reduce the fat intake of the family, and it is therefore not surprising that the market is filled with ovens that claim to achieve excellent cooking without addition of fats through obscure processes. Compared to them, NuWave's line of ovens does not make such strange claims, simply because the NuWave oven benefits, including the elimination of the need to add fats, are inherent in the ovens' very cooking mechanism.

Indeed, this innovative mechanism not only ensures good cooking without addition of fats, it also proactively removes fats from meats, etc. But how does this mechanism work? To explain this, we have prepared a short guide explaining the mechanism as well as the difference in fat reduction capacity between a NuWave oven and a conventional oven.

NuWave Oven Cooking Mechanism

Like all ovens, NuWave's range of ovens depends upon the diffusion of heat into the foodstuffs to achieve thorough cooking. Conventional ovens, unfortunately, have a lopsided heating mechanism that demands use of oils and grease to spread the heat effectively and thus ensure even cooking. However, NuWave's unique design and extremely efficient far infrared heating element ensure that all three heating processes – radiation, conduction and convection – are used in tandem to achieve a fast, thorough and most importantly – fat-less cooking.

This heating mechanism, called Triple Cooking Combo, ensures that the heat penetrates the food from one end to the other, with heating occurring at the centre of the foodstuff, before moving towards the surface. This ensures thorough and even cooking without the need for any conductinglike oil, thus eliminating the unhealthiest of ingredients from your kitchen.

NuWave Oven Removes Fats And Oils

NuWave oven benefits are not limited to elimination of the need to use oils. TCC also melts the fats and oils naturally present in foodstuffs and cause them to collect at the base of the oven. Though this feature will work regardless of the position in which the food is kept, it is advisable to place the fatty food on the grill, so as to create a small distance between it and the base of the oven. In this position, as the fats are melted, they trickle down to the bottom of the oven and are no longer part of the cooking procedure. Sufficient space at the base ensures that this most healthy of NuWave oven benefits is not compromised by the amount of fat contained in the foodstuff.

Indeed, research has shown that the removal of fats is greatest when the amount of fats is . In pork, for instance, the fat removal was found to be 250% more than that in a conventional oven. Similarly, 120% more beef fat was removed by NuWave ovens than by comparable conventional ovens.

As we can see, NuWave ovens eliminate the need for addition of fats and also remove fats from the fatty foods. This does not mean however, that the foods turn out to be devoid of flavor. Quite the opposite, since thorough and even cooking ensure that the natural flavors are retained and enhanced without the unpleasant tastes sometimes produced by excess addition of oils. Considered together, these NuWave oven benefits make these ovens the best candidates for inclusion in the kitchens of the modern health conscious families who do not wish to compromise on taste.

Here are some favorite recipes I've experimented with over the years and found excellent results. You may need to adjust you seasonings and cooking times to your own particular taste, and I would encourage you to experiment with variations on these basic recipes. Cooking should be an adventure!

The reason I wrote this book was because of how much I loved how the NuWave Oven saved me time cooking and preparing foods while still working a full time job, I had to feed a family of four every night!

I hope you enjoy the delicious possibilities your NuWave Oven provides – and the time it will save you in the kitchen.

ANGEL B. ANDERSON

CHAPTER 1

Using Your NuWave Oven (And NuWave Pro!)

Place food, fresh or frozen into the oven. There is no need to preheat or defrost. Try multi-layer cooking by placing different foods on each layer, saving both time and energy.

Set the Timer And Press Start.

NuWave Oven automatically cooks on power level HI so there is no need to select the power level unless you want to cook on a er temperature setting. Simply set the timer, press the"start" button and wait for your food to be done.

Enjoy Healthy & Delicious Meals in Minutes!

The oven will beep once the food is done. Enjoy delicious, gourmet meals done in the NuWave Oven!

CHAPTER 2

Snacks

NuWave ovens aren't just for cooking main meals or desserts – they are perfect for quick and easy snacks. Unlike microwaves, NuWave ovens can heat up pastries, pizzas and snacks without them resulting in a soggy mess. They can also make delicious toasties, warmed bagels, bruschetta and even boil an egg! Here are some reminders and some new ideas for you to try.

Toast

This is really where the accessories come into their own. If you purchase an accessory pack, a breakfast rack may come with it. This looks like a toast rack with some places for eggs. If you don't have this accessory, you could opt for an ovenproof toast rack and use it on the er NuWave Oven rack – make sure there is at least a 2cm gap between it and the NuWave Oven lid. You may have to cut the slices of bread in half to accommodate them.

Simply put your slices of bread on the rack.

Cook at HI for 6–8 minutes, until your toast reaches the desired color.

This is trial and error. When I first tried it, some of the slices were toasted but not golden – they still tasted the same but the odd slice lacked color. I experimented with the temperature setting until things improved.

Toasted Sandwich

If you want a toasted sandwich, place one slice with topping and one slice without topping side by side on the rack.

Cook at HI for 4–5 minutes until the toppings are bubbling.

Place the plain bread slice over the topped slice to form a sandwich and cook for a further 1–2 minutes if necessary.

Tomato and Onion Welsh Rarebit

A new take on the Welsh rarebit – perfect for using up any leftovers!

2–4 slices of bread
3–4 tablespoons milk
10g butter
100–150g mature cheese, grated
½ small onion, finely chopped (or a few spring onions)
1 tomato, chopped
1 teaspoon mustard
Black pepper to season
Preheat the NuWave Oven oven to HI.

Place the bread on the rack and cook for 2–3 minutes. Meanwhile, in a saucepan add the milk, butter, cheese, onion, tomato and mustard and stir until dissolved and thick. Season with black pepper. Be careful not to have the temperature too or it will stick and burn.

Take the bread out of the oven, turn it over and spoon on the cheese mixture. Season to taste. Place back on the rack and cook for another 3 minutes until golden and bubbling.

Serve with a side salad and some delicious chutney.

Bacon, Rocket and Tomato Deluxe

Extra virgin olive oil
2–4 rashers of bacon (depending on appetite!)
1–2 slices/portions of French bread or bagel
1–2 tomatoes, thickly sliced
Handful of rocket (or lettuce if you prefer)
Seasoning to taste
Preheat the NuWave Oven oven to HI.

Brush the bacon with a little olive oil and place on a grilling or browning tray on the est rack. Cook until the bacon almost reaches your desired crispiness (5–8 minutes, turning over halfway through).

Place the French bread or bagel alongside the bacon for a minute or two, as this will start to warm/toast one side of the bread.

Remove when ready and plate up: turn the bread over and place the bacon on top, cover with the tomato slices and finish with the rocket. Season and, if you are a fan of olive oil, drizzle with some extra virgin olive oil. Serve immediately!

Sardines in Tomato Sauce on Toast

2–4 slices of wholemeal or granary bread
120g tin of sardines in tomato sauce
Spring onions, chopped (optional)
Dollop of sundried tomatoes (optional)
Preheat the NuWave Oven oven to HI.

Place the bread on the rack and cook for 2–3 minutes. Meanwhile, remove the sardines from the tin and mash slightly (you can add some finely chopped spring onions and a dollop of sundried tomatoes if you like).

Remove the bread from the oven, turn the slices over and place the sardines on top.

Place back on the rack and cook for 3–4 minutes until golden and bubbling.

Serve with a side salad.

Bacon

Who can resist a bacon butty? You can cook your bacon without adding more fat in approximately 6–8 minutes using the NuWave Oven oven.

Place the bacon on the rack and set the temperature to HI.

Cook for 5 minutes, then turn over and cook for another 5 minutes or until the bacon reaches your desired crispiness.

Soft-boiled Eggs

You would not really think that the NuWave Oven oven could be used to boil an egg, but you will be surprised. You can place the egg directly onto the rack, or you could opt for the breakfast rack as an optional accessory.

2–4 slices of bread
2–3 eggs
10g butter
Preheat the NuWave Oven oven to HI.
Place the eggs on the rack or breakfast rack.
Cook for 6 minutes to achieve a soft-boiled egg. Take care when removing the eggs from the oven as they will be very hot.

Note: This did not work when I first tried it. I discovered that you really have to preheat the oven and it is best if the eggs are at room temperature. If they have been stored in a cold fridge you may have to cook them for a minute or two more. You will soon find the timing to suit your preference.

Hard-boiled Eggs

Preheat the NuWave Oven oven to HI.
Place the eggs on the rack or breakfast rack.
Cook for 10 minutes to achieve a hardboiled egg. Take care when removing the eggs from the oven as they will be very hot.

Tuna Melt Panini

Create your own café-favourite snack in your NuWave Oven.

1 small tin of tuna
Mayonnaise
Cheddar cheese, grated
Seasoning to taste
1–2 panini rolls

In a bowl, mix the tuna, mayonnaise (enough to reach a creamy consistency) and Cheddar to taste. Season well.

Preheat the NuWave Oven oven using the HI setting.

Slice open the panini rolls and toast for 2–3 minutes. Fill with the tuna mixture. Close the panini.

Place on the rack and cook for 4–6 minutes until golden and the tuna and cheese mixture has started to melt.

Serve with a side salad and tortilla chips.

Muffin Pizzas

These are so easy to make, it makes you wonder why we bother messing around with pizza dough. Kids love them if you get them to decorate the tops to resemble faces. Feel free to use whatever topping you prefer; this is a basic recipe using just cheese and tomato pasta sauce – the rest is up to you!

1–2 muffins, sliced in half, horizontally
2–4 spoonfuls of pasta sauce
Mature Cheddar, grated
Black pepper to season

Place the muffins ready to assemble on a worktop or tray. Add a layer of the pasta sauce (my cheat's way!) fooled by any other ingredients you require and finish with a generous handful of grated cheese. Season to taste.

Place the muffins directly on the rack (or on a browning tray if you prefer). Set the temperature to HI and cook until golden and bubbling (this should only take 5–7 minutes).

Serve immediately.

Cheese, Sundried Tomatoes and Rocket Bagel

This is my favourite bagel combination. Perfect with a lovely sesame or seeded bagel.

1–2 bagels

Cheddar cheese, grated or sliced

3–6 sundried tomatoes (drained of oil)

Rocket

Slice open the bagels and place inside upwards on the est rack of your NuWave Oven. Set the oven to HI. Cook for 4–5 minutes until they start to brown.

Remove and add the cheese, sundried tomatoes and rocket. Season to taste.

Serve immediately while still warm!

Fresh Garlic Bread

You can make your own garlic bread by foling this basic recipe.

French stick

1 tablespoon butter

1 or 2 crushed garlic cloves

Sprinkle of mixed herbs

Partially slice a French stick into 2–3cm thick slices (making sure you don't cut right through to the base).

Mix the butter with the garlic and a sprinkle of mixed herbs. Thickly spread this garlic butter in between the slices of bread.

Place on a baking tray, first making sure it fits into your NuWave Oven oven.

Place the tray on the rack and turn the NuWave Oven to HI. Cook for 5–8 minutes, until golden.

To serve, simply al the diners to tear the bread slices.

Variation: Try spreading with either green or red pesto instead of garlic butter.

Frozen Garlic Bread

Place the bread, partially sliced, on a baking tray, first making sure it fits into your NuWave Oven oven.

Place the tray on the rack and turn the oven on to HI.. Cook for 5–8 minutes, until bread is golden. If baking the bread from frozen, add an extra 5–8 minutes.

To serve, simply al the diners to tear the bread slices.

Warming Naan Bread

Naan bread is delicious with curries and Indian meals. You can now buy ready-made naan bread and the NuWave Oven oven is a great tool for warming it.

Sprinkle the naan bread with a little cold water.

Place on the rack and cook for 5–8 minutes at HI.

Serve immediately.

Frozen Pizza

Refer to your oven manufacturer's instructions for more information.

Place the pizza (frozen or defrosted) on the rack. If you have the NuWave Oven accessory pack, you could place it on the browning tray. If not, place it directly on the rack or use a pizza tray.

You may want to place the upper rack, upside down, on top of the pizza for the first 10 minutes. This prevents the pizza toppings from lifting with the force of the fan – this is particularly advisable if your pizza has lots of loose toppings. The Flavorwave Turbo Platinum has three fan settings, so you could opt to choose the fan setting which avoids needing to cover the top of the pizza.

Set the temperature to HI and cook for 10–15 minutes, until golden.

Frozen Oven Chips

If you have children or teenagers in the house, there will come a time when they'll want you to cook some oven chips. The NuWave Oven cooks these in approximately 20 minutes.

Turn the NuWave Oven to HI.

Place the oven chips (frozen or defrosted) on a baking tray on the rack. Alternatively, you can place them on the bottom of the NuWave Oven oven if you prefer.

I sprinkle the chips with a touch of paprika and a tiny dash of olive oil to add flavour and prevent the chips from becoming too dry.

Cook for 20–25 minutes, turning occasionally if you feel like it, until they are golden.

Toasted Cheese and Ham Croissants

As with the panini, bruschetta and toasted sandwiches, this recipe is designed to show you what you can do with the NuWave Oven. Feel free to change the ingredients to suit your palate. Why not try a sweet filling? One of my children's favourites is chocolate spread with slices of banana.

1–2 croissants
Mature cheese
2–3 slices of ham
Seasoning to taste

Preheat the NuWave Oven using the preheat setting or set the temperature to HI.

Slice the croissants in half horizontally and fill them with cheese and ham.

Place the filled croissants on the rack and cook for 3–6 minutes until crispy and the cheese has started to melt.

Serve immediately.

Crumpets

There is nothing like the taste of hot, buttered crumpets. You could add some crumbled stilton for a savoury variation – yummy! Set oven to HI.

Place the crumpets on the rack and grill until they reach your preferred toasting.

If you are adding a topping, do so after the crumpets have started to brown and not at the beginning of the process.

Serve hot.

Baked Camembert

I'm a bit embarrassed to call this a recipe, but once you have tasted it you will understand why it is a favorite.

SERVES 2–4

250g whole camembert cheese

If your camembert comes in a wooden box, remove all packaging before placing the camembert back into the box. Alternatively, wrap the cheese in foil and place on a baking tray. I actually have a little ovenware pot that came with some camembert and which I reuse.

There is no need to preheat the oven. Simply place the camembert, in foil or an ovenware pot, on the middle rack and bake for 10 minutes at HI.

Serve with a selection of vegetable sticks, crusty bread or lightly steamed asparagus spears – or all three!

CHAPTER 3

Meat

The NuWave Oven can cook meat quicker than the conventional oven, though you have to be careful to get your timings right. Too long and the tops of the joint or bird will burn, while the middle may remain raw or undercooked. I would advise using an oven thermometer to test your meat, particularly poultry or joints of meat until you are more confident.

When meat is placed on the rack, it allows the juices and fats to drain away – therefore making the meat healthier. I have found that meat does tend to be very tender and moist when cooked in the NuWave Oven ... unless you overcook it!

If you are cooking a joint of meat you can cook it as you would do in a conventional oven – roughly 20 minutes on HI per 500g and adding 5-10 minutes to the end of the cooking time as you increase the amount of meat.

As with all foods cooked in the NuWave Oven make sure there is adequate space between the element and the food – ideally at least 2–3cm. The nearer the food is to the element, the more likely it is to burn or cook too quickly. If you are concerned, wrap some foil over the food for the first half of the cooking time, but do make sure the foil is secured well as the power of the fan could lift it.

Parma-wrapped Chilli Chicken

A very simple dish that takes minutes to prepare.

SERVES 2

1–2 tablespoons quark or fat cream cheese
½–1 red chilli, finely chopped
½ teaspoon chili powder
Few drops of Tabasco sauce to taste (optional)
Seasoning to taste
2 chicken breasts
4 slices Parma ham
Olive oil

Preheat the NuWave Oven using the preheat setting or set the temperature to HI.

Place the quark or cream cheese in a bowl and mix in the chili and Tabasco sauce until combined. Season to taste.

Using a sharp knife, cut a slit in each chicken breast to form a pocket. Stuff the pockets with the creamed mixture.

Wrap securely with Parma ham. Place seam-side down on a greased ovenproof dish. Drizzle with olive oil and season to taste.

Place on the rack and cook for 20–30 minutes until the chicken is cooked.

Balsamic Steaks

This is a really simple dish – just remember to marinate either overnight or for at least 2 hours before cooking.

SERVES 2

1 tablespoon brown sugar
2–3 garlic cloves, crushed
1 teaspoon mild/ chilli powder
1 teaspoon paprika
3 tablespoons balsamic vinegar
1 tablespoon olive oil
Seasoning to taste
2 lean steaks

In a bowl, mix the sugar, garlic, chilli powder, paprika, balsamic vinegar, olive oil and seasoning to form a paste.

Dip the steaks into the mixture and leave coated overnight or for at least 2 hours before cooking.

When ready to cook, heat the NuWave Oven to HI.. Place the steaks on the rack and grill on both sides until done to your desired taste.

Serve with a green salad.

Pan-roasted Vegetables and Chicken Breasts Wrapped in Parma Ham

A simple one-pot dish.

SERVES 2

200g new potatoes, washed and halved
1 red onion, deseeded and cut into wedges
1 red pepper, cut into wedges
8–12 cherry tomatoes
3–4 cloves of garlic, left whole
Olive oil
2–3 sprigs of thyme
2 chicken breasts
2–4 slices of Parma ham
Paprika
Seasoning to taste

Place the vegetables and garlic cloves in an oiled ovenproof dish or roasting tin, first making sure it fits well in your NuWave Oven. Drizzle with oil and add the sprigs of thyme. Toss well to ensure everything is evenly coated.

Place on the middle rack. Set the temperature to HI and cook for 10 minutes.

Meanwhile, sprinkle the chicken breasts with paprika and wrap in the Parma ham. Season to taste.

Remove the NuWave Oven's lid and make a gap in the vegetables for the chicken. Carefully place (don't burn yourself) the wrapped chicken breasts, seam-side down, among the vegetables. Drizzle with olive oil.

Replace the lid and cook at HI for 20–30 minutes, or until the chicken is cooked to your liking. If the vegetables start to brown too much, you can cover the dish with foil, but the tomatoes and peppers become very sweet when they start to darken which adds to the flavor.

Serve when the chicken is cooked to your satisfaction.

Garlic and Rosemary Chicken Parcels

A simple dish with great flavors that can be prepared in advance.

SERVES 2

Olive oil
2–4 slices of red onion
2 chicken breasts
Chicken seasoning (I use Schwartz No Added Salt Chicken seasoning)
10g butter
3–4 cloves of garlic, crushed
1 teaspoon freshly-chopped rosemary
Seasoning to taste
4 tablespoons white wine or vermouth

Measure and cut some foil double the size of each chicken breast. The foil also needs to be double thickness.

Brush the centre of each piece of foil with olive oil.

Place 1–2 slices of red onion on top of the olive oil. Place the chicken breasts on top of the onion. Season with the chicken seasoning.

In a small bowl or cup, mix the butter with the garlic. Place a spoonful of this butter mixture onto each of the chicken fillets.

Sprinkle with the chopped rosemary and season to taste.

Pull the sides of the foil up to form a bowl shape, before adding the wine or vermouth. Then scrunch the foil securely closed and place on a baking tray. You can either leave the chicken to marinate until you are ready to cook, or cook it immediately.

Place on the middle rack and set the NuWave Oven to HI. Cook for 10 minutes.

Remove the NuWave Oven's lid and very carefully unwrap the foil, exposing the chicken but leaving the foil edges to avoid the juices leaking. Cook for another 10–15 minutes or until the chicken is cooked to your liking.

Serve with sautéed potatoes and steamed seasonal vegetables.

Beef and Ale Casserole

This is a traditional casserole that benefits from a s cook. You can cook this on the hob if you prefer but the NuWave Oven works well. If your NuWave Oven has a digital timer you can, of course, set it to suit your timing, but if it has a dial timer (which is more common) you will have to reset this after 60 minutes.

SERVES 2

350g shin of beef or stewing steak, diced
1 tablespoon plain flour
½ teaspoon paprika
Seasoning to taste
2 tablespoons olive oil
1 small onion, finely chopped
2 small to -sized carrots, diced
1 stick of celery, diced
175ml real ale or stout
1 tablespoon tomato purée
2 teaspoons brown sugar
300ml beef stock
Bouquet garni (thyme, parsley, bay leaf)
100g mushrooms, chopped
10g butter

If your meat is not already diced, cut it into chunks and remove any excess fat.

Place the flour, paprika and seasoning in a bowl or freezer bag. Add the meat, shake and coat until it is covered well.

Heat the oil in a sauté pan on the hob and brown the meat on all sides. Then place the meat into a casserole dish.

(Make sure that your casserole dish fits in the NuWave Oven. Ideally choose one with a lid for later use, but if your dish does not have a lid you could instead use an extension ring or a double layer of foil, securely folded.)

Using the same pan as you browned the meat in, add the onion, carrots and celery and cook for about 5 minutes on a / heat before adding the ale, tomato purée and sugar. Stir well, making sure you also scrape up any meat juices or leftovers as you go. Once heated, add this to the meat and top up with the beef stock. Combine well.

Add *bouquet garni* and salt and pepper to the casserole. Cover the dish with a lid (or double layer of tin foil held securely) and place on the rack. Turn the NuWave Oven to HI. and cook for 1 hour.

After the hour, fry the mushrooms in butter on the hob until tender and add to the casserole.

Turn the heat up to HI and continue to cook for another 15 minutes.

Serve with fluffy mashed potatoes and seasonal vegetables.

Creamy Chicken Casserole

SERVES 2

     Olive oil
2 chicken ts, depending on appetite!
1 small onion, peeled and roughly chopped
1 garlic clove, crushed
1 leek, finely chopped
75ml white wine
250ml chicken stock
Seasoning
1 bay leaf
75g frozen peas
50ml double cream
Small handful of finely chopped tarragon
1 teaspoon cornflour (optional)

Brown the chicken ts to a nice golden colour. To do this there are two options: hob or NuWave Oven.

* Hob: Simply add olive oil to the pan and, on a / heat, cook the chicken on both sides until golden. Remove and place in your casserole dish (make sure it fits in your NuWave Oven!), along with the onion, garlic and leeks.

* NuWave Oven: Place the chicken in a pan on the rack and brush with oil. Add the onion, garlic and leeks to the pan as you can soften them at the same time. Set the temperature to HI and cook the chicken on both sides until golden. Remove from the oven and place the chicken and vegetables into your casserole dish (making sure it fits into your NuWave Oven).

Pour the wine and chicken stock over the chicken ts. Season and add the bay leaf.

Cover the casserole dish with a lid (or if your dish does not have a lid use an extension ring or a double layer of foil, held securely) and cook in the NuWave Oven at HI. for 1 hour.

When the hour is up, add the frozen peas, cream and tarragon. Combine well. If, at this stage your sauce is too thin, you could mix a teaspoon of cornflour with a little water and combine it into your casserole. It will thicken as it cooks. Cook for another 15 minutes.

Serve with new potatoes and seasonal vegetables.

Chicken Breast stuffed with Cream Cheese and Mustard Sauce

SERVES 2

2 chicken breasts
1 tablespoon olive oil
3 tablespoons cream cheese
1 tablespoon Dijon mustard
2 teaspoons chopped chives
Sea salt
Black pepper

Wash the chicken breasts before cutting almost in half horizontally. Place on a sheet of greaseproof paper or clingfilm. With a rolling pin or meat mallet, flatten until thin.

Mix the cream cheese with the mustard and chives and season to taste. Spread this mixture over the open chicken breasts.

Carefully roll each breast up like a Swiss roll and secure with a wooden (previously soaked) cocktail stick. Place on a greased browning tray.

Set the NuWave Oven oven to HI. and place the tray on the rack. Cook for 15–20 minutes until breasts are golden.

Serve with new potatoes and seasonal vegetables.

Spicy Meatballs with Rich Tomato Sauce and Spaghetti

This meal can be cooked in advance. The two stages – the meatballs and the rich sauce – can both be prepared in advance and reheated when needed. If you are opting to do this, fol stages one and two and refrigerate until ready to cook. You can also freeze the meatballs. The sauce is best kept in a sealed container in your fridge for no more than three days.

SERVES 2

225g lean beef or lamb mince
2 cloves of garlic, chopped
½ chilli, finely chopped
½ teaspoon ground cumin
Zest of ½ lemon
Sea salt
Black pepper
200g cherry tomatoes
2–3 cloves of garlic, finely chopped
1 small red onion, finely chopped
½ red pepper, deseeded and chopped
Olive oil
Balsamic vinegar
1 teaspoon sugar
1 teaspoon dried or small handful of freshly chopped oregano
100–150g spaghetti, depending on appetite
Grated parmesan to garnish

Place the mince into a large bowl and add 2 cloves of chopped garlic, chilli, cumin and lemon zest. Season to taste with sea salt and black pepper. Mix well and shape into balls. Leave these in the fridge for 10 minutes or until needed. (You can also freeze them on a baking sheet at this stage. Once frozen they can be transferred into a freezer bag, which prevents them from sticking to each other when frozen.)

Meanwhile, make the rich tomato sauce. Place the

29

tomatoes, 2–3 cloves of finely chopped garlic, red onion and red pepper in an ovenproof dish. Drizzle with olive oil and a dash of balsamic vinegar. Sprinkle with sea salt, sugar and some dried or fresh oregano. Place on the rack at HI. and cook for 15 minutes (or 30 if you are preparing the sauce for later use).

When you are ready to cook the meatballs, transfer them to a greased baking dish or browning tray. (First defrost the meatballs if they are frozen.) Place on the rack and set the temperature to HI. Place the tomato mixture on the rack so it can continue to cook or reheat if it has been prepared in advance. Bake until the meatballs are browned and cooked, turning occasionally. This should take no more than 15 minutes.

While this is cooking, prepare the spaghetti as per the manufacturer's instructions.

To serve, place the meatballs on a bed of spaghetti and pour over the tomato sauce. Garnish with a sprinkle of freshly grated parmesan.

Fruity Chicken

SERVES 2

Olive oil
2 chicken breasts
Dash of paprika
1 small red onion, chopped
2–3 rashers of thick smoked bacon or lardons, thickly diced
4 no-soak prunes, chopped roughly
4 no-soak apricots, chopped roughly
1 teaspoon freshly chopped rosemary
150ml chicken stock
100ml white wine
Sea salt
Black pepper

In a deep ovenproof dish, add the olive oil and chicken breasts. Sprinkle the chicken with a dash of paprika. Place on the est rack you can fit the dish onto (this may be the rack depending on the height of your dish). Set the temperature to 210°C and brown the chicken on both sides.

Once browned, add the onion and bacon and continue to cook for another 5–8 minutes until the onion and bacon start to soften.

Add the remaining ingredients and season with sea salt and black pepper. Cover with a lid or a double layer of tin foil (firmly secured) and turn the temperature down to HI. Cook for 20–25 minutes.

Serve with fluffy mashed potato and seasonal vegetables.

Red Pesto Chicken Parcels

SERVES 2

> 2 chicken breasts
> Butter
> 2–4 teaspoons red pesto
> 1 small red onion, sliced
> 2 tablespoons white wine
> Seasoning

Cut out 2 double-thickness squares of foil, twice the size of each chicken breast. Grease each double-thickness square with a little butter.

Place one chicken breast in the middle of each square. Add 1–2 teaspoons of red pesto to each chicken breast. Cover with some onion slices.

Drizzle with a tablespoon of white wine. Season well and secure into a parcel.

Preheat the NuWave Oven using the preheat setting or turn on to HI.. Place the chicken parcels on the rack and cook for 20–25 minutes until cooked.

Beefy Stuffed Onions with Goat's Cheese Topping

This is a lovely dish that is also very filling. If you are vegetarian you can opt to use veggie or Quorn mince instead of beef. This dish can be prepared in advance and reheated.

SERVES 2

> 2 large onions, peeled
> Knob of butter
> Olive oil
> 175g lean minced beef
> 2 tomatoes, finely chopped
> 1 tablespoon tomato purée

50ml red wine (optional)
2 cloves of garlic, crushed
1–2 sprigs of thyme
1 teaspoon freshly chopped rosemary
Sea salt
Black pepper
100g goat's cheese

Boil the onions in a pan of water for 5 minutes. Drain and leave until they are cool enough to handle.

Cut off the top of each onion and remove the inside leaving a thick outer shell. Chop the discarded onion and leave to one side as you will need this later.

Spread some butter inside the onions and place into a greased ovenproof dish.

Heat a little olive oil in a sauté pan and cook the chopped onion until it softens. Add the mince and continue to cook until it has browned.

Once browned, add the chopped tomatoes, tomato purée, red wine (optional), garlic, thyme, rosemary and seasoning. Cook for another couple of minutes until thoroughly combined and heated through.

Spoon the mixture into the onion shells. Finish with a thick layer of goat's cheese, foled by a sprinkle of black pepper.

Place on the rack at HI and bake for 20–25 minutes until the onion is soft and the goat's cheese is golden and bubbling.

Serve with a green salad.

Chicken with Mustard Sauce

SERVES 2

Olive oil
2 chicken breasts
1 heaped dessertspoon butter
1 dessertspoon cornflour
250ml hot chicken stock
2–3 heaped teaspoons wholegrain mustard (depending on your taste)
150ml double cream
Seasoning

Place the chicken breasts in an oiled ovenproof dish. Place this on the rack and cook at HI., turning the chicken until it is golden on both sides.

Meanwhile, melt the butter in a pan. Add the flour and make a paste. Add the stock, gently whisking all the time. The sauce should be thick and shiny.

Remove from the heat and add the mustard, cream and seasoning. Pour the sauce over the browned chicken.

Turn the temperature down to HI. and cook for another 15 minutes or until the chicken is cooked through to your satisfaction.

Serve with sauté potatoes and seasonal vegetables.

Feta, Pancetta and Onion Puff

This is a light dish with a consistency similar to soufflés. It makes a nice one-pot, supper-time dish.

SERVES 2

50g fresh breadcrumbs
275ml milk
1 small onion, halved or quartered
1 bay leaf
1 teaspoon wholegrain mustard
2 eggs, separated
75g pancetta, chopped
50g feta cheese, crumbled
½ teaspoon dried thyme or small handful of freshly chopped thyme
Seasoning to taste

Place the breadcrumbs in a bowl. Place the milk, onion and bay leaf in a pan and bring to the boil.

Remove the onion (leaving it to one side) and bay leaf and stir in the mustard. Pour this over the breadcrumbs and leave to stand for 20–30 minutes.

Separate the eggs. Mix the egg yolks and all other ingredients (leaving the egg whites to one side) together with the soaked breadcrumbs.

Chop the remaining onion finely and add to the mixture.

Beat the egg whites until light and fluffy. Fold into the mixture carefully.

Pour this into a well-greased ovenproof dish.

Preheat the NuWave Oven oven using the preheat setting or set the temperature to HI.. Bake on the rack for 20–25 minutes.

Serve with a green salad.

Pesto Pork

Perfect for the NuWave Oven – quick, simple and tastes great. Serve with a selection of roasted vegetables.

SERVES 2

2 pork chops or loin steaks
½ small tub of cream cheese
2–3 teaspoons pesto
50g wholemeal breadcrumbs
25g parmesan cheese, grated
Seasoning to taste

Preheat the NuWave Oven using the preheat setting or set the temperature to HI.

Place the chops or steaks on the grill tray. Grill on the rack for 3–4 minutes each side until they are almost cooked. Remove and put to one side.

Mix the cream cheese and the pesto together thoroughly.

In another bowl, mix the breadcrumbs and parmesan together and season to taste.

Pour the pesto mix onto the pork, ensuring the tops are covered. Sprinkle on the breadcrumb mixture to finish.

Place back in the NuWave Oven on the rack and cook until the topping is golden and bubbling. This should take no more than 5 minutes.

Spring Chicken Casserole

This is the perfect dish to use up any of the lovely spring vegetables. Sometimes spring can still be a bit chilly so there is nothing better than a delicious, warming evening meal. This recipe is perfect.

SERVES 2

2 chicken breasts
½ teaspoon paprika
Sea salt
Black pepper
Olive oil
150g new potatoes, finely sliced
1 small carrot, finely diced
½ bunch of spring onions, chopped
150ml white wine or vermouth
250–350ml chicken stock, warmed
Small handful of fresh tarragon
50g French beans
½ small head of broccoli, cut into small florets
50g peas
2–3 tablespoons crème fraîche

Rub the chicken breasts with paprika. Season to taste. Place them in an oiled ovenproof dish and finish with an extra drizzle of oil.

Add the sliced potatoes, carrot and spring onions.

Place on the rack and set the temperature to HI. Cook for 15 minutes.

Meanwhile, prepare the other ingredients. Once the 15 minutes are up, add the remaining ingredients apart from the crème fraîche. Combine well.

Cover with a lid or double layer of foil and cook at HI for another 30 minutes.

Remove from the oven and stir in the crème fraîche.

Serve with crusty bread and salad.

Moussaka

SERVES 2

    1 aubergine, sliced
    Olive oil
    1 small onion, finely chopped
    1 clove garlic, crushed
    200g lamb mince
    ½ tin chopped tomatoes
    1 teaspoons tomato purée
    1 teaspoon dried mint
    1 teaspoon ground cinnamon
    Seasoning to taste
    150ml fat crème fraîche
    30g mature Cheddar or parmesan cheese, grated

Place the aubergine slices in a pan of boiling water for 2 minutes. Remove and pat dry. Leave to one side.

Meanwhile, heat a little olive oil in a sauté pan and fry the onion and garlic. Add the lamb mince and cook until brown.

Add the tomatoes, tomato purée, mint, cinnamon and seasoning and cook for another 2–3 minutes.

Select your ovenproof dish – I normally use a Pyrex or small lasagne dish for this. Make sure it fits into your NuWave Oven. Preheat the NuWave Oven using the preheat setting or set to HI.

Place a layer of mince in the dish, foled by a layer of aubergine. Continue alternating mince and aubergine, finishing with a layer of mince.

Mix the crème fraîche with the grated cheese and pour over the final layer of mince. Garnish with a sprinkle of parmesan.

Place on the rack and cook for 20–25 minutes until bubbling.

Italian Chicken One Pot

A very simple dish. Why not prepare this in advance and leave it covered in the fridge until you are ready to cook – perfect for a lovely meal after a day at work.

SERVES 2

Olive oil
2 chicken breasts
Paprika
1 small red onion, thickly sliced or cut into wedges
2–3 cloves of garlic, halved
1 pepper, cut into thick wedges
4 sundried tomatoes (in oil), halved
50g thick pancetta, diced
6–8 ripe vine tomatoes, whole
6–8 new potatoes, sliced
2 sprigs of thyme
Sea salt
Black pepper

Drizzle olive oil into a roasting tin or ovenproof dish. Score the chicken breasts with a sharp knife. Rub with a little olive oil and sprinkle with paprika. Place the chicken in the roasting dish.

Add the remaining ingredients, ensuring they are evenly distributed in the dish. Finish with a drizzle of olive oil and season with sea salt and black pepper.

Place on the rack and set the temperature to HI. Cook for 20–30 minutes or until the chicken is cooked to your liking. Serve immediately.

Mediterranean-style Tortilla

This is an ideal dish for using up any leftover vegetables – anything goes, so experiment!

SERVES 2

2–3 eggs, beaten

½ bunch of spring onions, finely chopped

½ red pepper, diced or thinly sliced

3 rashers pancetta, diced

2–3 sundried tomatoes, chopped

25g parmesan, grated

Small handful of fresh herbs (basil, oregano or thyme would suit)

Seasoning to taste

Preheat your NuWave oven using your preheat setting or set the temperature to HI.

In a large bowl, add the eggs and beat well. Add the remaining ingredients and combine. Pour into a well-greased ovenproof dish.

Place on the rack and cook for 20–25 minutes until firm.

Serve hot or cold with salad.

Lamb Biryani

Olive oil
350g lamb, cubed
1 small onion, diced
1 clove of garlic, crushed
½ teaspoon ground cinnamon
½ teaspoon ground cardamom
½ teaspoon ground cloves
½ teaspoon curry powder
125ml plain Greek yoghurt
2 tomatoes, diced
120g long grain rice
Toasted almonds to sprinkle

In a sauté pan, add the oil and heat until hot. Add the lamb, onion and garlic and cook until the lamb starts to brown and the onion starts to soften.

Add the spices and cook for a couple of minutes before adding the yoghurt and tomatoes. Combine well and gently cook on a heat.

Meanwhile cook the rice following the manufacturer's instructions. (I normally add 1¼ water to rice, bring to the boil and leave simmering for a couple of minutes before popping a lid on and removing completely from the heat. Leave to stand for 10–12 minutes. Fluff up using a fork.)

When the rice is done, place a layer in the bottom of your ovenproof dish. Fol this with a layer of the lamb mixture. Continue until you have used up all the ingredients.

Cover with foil and place on the rack. Turn the temperature to HI. and cook for 20 minutes.

Garnish with the toasted almonds before serving.

Chicken, Mushroom and Bacon Lasagne

As with all lasagne cooked in the NuWave Oven, you can speed up the cooking process by using fresh lasagne sheets or parboiling packet ones before adding to the dish.

SERVES 2

Olive oil
125g mushrooms, sliced (a mixture of different types is good)
4 rashers lean bacon, diced
Knob of butter
1 tablespoon plain flour or cornflour
200ml milk
125g cooked chicken, chopped
Black pepper
Sea salt
200g tinned tomatoes, drained and chopped
½ teaspoon dried mixed herbs
Lasagne sheets
125ml Greek yoghurt
1 small egg, beaten
1 level tablespoon grated parmesan cheese

Note: Ideal for using up any cooked chicken.

Place the olive oil into a sauté pan and cook the mushrooms and bacon for 5–8 minutes. Remove from the heat.

Melt the butter in a heavy-based saucepan. Add the flour and stir well with a wooden spoon. Gradually add the milk and bring sly to the boil, stirring all the time. You may want to add more milk if you think the sauce is becoming too thick.

Add the chicken, mushrooms and bacon to the sauce. Stir well before seasoning with black pepper and sea salt.

In another bowl, combine the tomatoes, herbs and seasoning.

Start to layer your lasagne by placing some of the

tomato mixture in the base, foled by lasagne sheets, followed by the chicken mixture. Continue, finishing with lasagne sheets on the top.

Mix the yoghurt and the egg and spread over the top. Sprinkle with parmesan and season with black pepper.

Place the lasagne on the rack. Turn the temperature to HI. and cook for about 40 minutes (less if you have parboiled the lasagne sheets or used fresh). If it starts to darken on top, cover securely with tin foil.

Serve with potato wedges and green salad.

Garlicky Chicken

This really is garlicky, so if you don't like garlic avoid this dish. You can use whatever chicken pieces you prefer. I like chicken breasts but that is just personal preference. Prepare this dish up to a day in advance to al the flavors to really develop.

SERVES 2

½ bulb of garlic, cloves peeled
150ml olive oil
Juice and zest of 1 lemon
2 tablespoons crème fraîche
½ teaspoon mustard
Black pepper
Sea salt
2–4 chicken breasts (depending on appetite!)

Using a food processor or electric mini chopping gadget, combine the garlic, olive oil, lemon juice and zest and whizz until it forms a smooth creamy paste. Add the crème fraîche and mustard before seasoning with black pepper and sea salt.

Wash the chicken pieces and place them in a greased ovenproof dish, just big enough to hold the chicken. Pour over the sauce, ensuring the chicken is well coated. Cover with a double layer of tin foil and place in the fridge to marinate.

Remove from the fridge in time for the chicken to be at room temperature when you are ready to cook.

Once ready, simply place the dish (with foil still intact) on the rack and cook at HI. for 30–40 minutes until the chicken is tender and cooked to your requirements.

Serve with green vegetables and mini roast potatoes.

Tender Chili Chicken in Breadcrumbs

This is a really lovely dish, made all the better by marinating for at least an hour, or overnight, before adding the breadcrumbs. (Remember to stock your freezer with breadcrumbs made from any stale bread you have lurking in your bread bin. Bag them in freezer bags ready for toppings, coatings or even an indulgent treacle tart!)

SERVES 2

2 chicken breasts
1 tablespoon olive oil
1–2 tablespoons white wine or vermouth
2 cloves garlic, peeled
½ red chilli
Juice of ½ lemon
Sea salt
Black pepper
60g fresh breadcrumbs
Pinch dried thyme
Pinch cayenne pepper
20g grated parmesan

Flatten the chicken breasts using a rolling pin or wooden kitchen mallet. You need to get them as thin as possible.

Place the olive oil, white wine or vermouth, garlic, chilli, lemon juice and seasoning in your food processor and whizz until smooth. Pour over the chicken, cover with foil or clingfilm and place in the fridge for at least an hour to marinate.

Remove the chicken from the fridge so that it reaches room temperature before cooking. Meanwhile, place the remaining ingredients in a bowl and combine well. Sprinkle the breadcrumb mix over the chicken pieces, pressing down well where you can.

Place the chicken on the rack and set the temperature to

HI.. Cook for 15–20 minutes.

Serve with a crisp green salad and, for an extra chilli hit, some sweet chilli sauce.

Spicy Polenta Chicken

I had never cooked with polenta until I found a recipe using Italian flavors. Polenta can be a bit tasteless so I would advise, if you like your food to be tasty, seasoning well and using some spices. I love the flavour of coriander seeds and polenta, just like sweet potato, really works well with it.

SERVES 2

1–2 teaspoons coriander seeds
1 red chilli, finely chopped
2 cloves garlic, finely chopped
½–1 teaspoon sweet curry powder
400g ready-to-use polenta
1 small red onion, cut into wedges
6–8 cherry tomatoes, whole
Small handful of coriander leaves
2 boneless chicken breasts
2 tablespoons natural Greek yoghurt
Black pepper
Sea salt
Olive oil

Using a pestle and mortar, grind the coriander seeds. Add half the chopped chilli, the garlic and sweet curry powder and combine well.

In a roasting dish or deep baking tray, crumble the polenta into bite-sized chunks. Spread this evenly around the base of the dish. Sprinkle the spice mixture evenly over the polenta. Finish by interspersing the onion, tomatoes and a few coriander leaves among the polenta.

Use a sharp knife to gently score the top of each chicken breast – 3 or 4 lines will be perfect. Place the chicken in the dish with the polenta. Carefully place the Greek yoghurt over the top of the chicken to form a coating.

Season the whole dish with black pepper and sea salt and finish with a generous drizzle of olive oil.

Place the dish on the rack and set the temperature to 220°C. Cook for 20–30 minutes until the chicken is golden.

Serve immediately.

Pan-roasted Breakfast

Don't think this is only suitable for breakfast – it is ideal for a lovely supper, especially when you require comfort food.

SERVES 2

1 punnet of cherry tomatoes
1–2 cloves garlic
½ pack of thick bacon, roughly chopped
Olive oil
Sea salt
Black pepper
2 large eggs
1 tablespoon chopped parsley

Place the tomatoes, garlic and bacon in an ovenproof dish (first making sure it fits in your NuWave Oven). Sprinkle with olive oil, sea salt and black pepper.

Place on the rack at HI. for 10–12 minutes.

Remove from the oven. Make two spaces evenly in the mixture and crack an egg into each space.

Cover the dish with foil or a lid and bake for a further 10–15 minutes until the eggs are cooked to your taste.

Remove from the oven, garnish with chopped parsley and serve immediately with warm crusty bread.

Lemon and Ginger Pork Chops

You will need to marinate these, ideally for around 3–4 hours to get a lovely moist and flavorsome chop. Once marinated, simply pop in the oven and cook for 20 minutes – so easy!

SERVES 2

30ml olive oil

½ bunch of spring onions, chopped

Juice and rind of 1 lemon

2cm knuckle of fresh ginger, finely chopped

1 clove of garlic, crushed

Small handful of fresh coriander, finely chopped

100ml Greek yoghurt (I use Total as it holds during cooking)

Seasoning to taste

2 pork chops

Extra coriander leaves to garnish

Mix all the ingredients together apart from the chops. Add the chops ensuring they are fully covered. (You can either do this in the bowl you made the marinade in, or place the marinade in a freezer bag, add the chops and shake well to cover.) Place the marinating chops in the fridge for at least 4 hours.

Once ready to cook, place the chops in the base of an oiled ovenproof dish. Pour over the remaining marinade.

Preheat the NuWave Oven to HI.

Place on the rack and cook for 20 minutes, or until the chops are cooked to your desired taste.

Serve with a garnish of coriander leaves.

One-pot Italian Lamb Steaks

This is a really easy dish. You can prepare it in advance and leave in the fridge to marinate, or simply throw it together 30 minutes before you want to eat.

SERVES 2

½ tin of tomatoes
100ml red wine
50g cherry tomatoes
1 small red onion, cut into thick slices or wedges
½ red pepper, cut into thick slices
1–3 cloves of garlic, whole
50g black olives, halved
2–3 sprigs of thyme
Sea salt
Black pepper
2 lamb steaks

In an ovenproof dish, add all the ingredients apart from the lamb, and combine until evenly coated and distributed. Place the lamb in among the vegetables and press down until it is covered slightly with the juice. Place in the fridge, covered, until needed.

When you are ready to cook, preheat the NuWave Oven to HI.

Place the dish on the rack and cook for 20–30 minutes until the lamb is cooked to your satisfaction.

Serve immediately with crusty bread and a green salad.

Sweet & Chilli Chops

A friend passed this recipe on to me, I hope you enjoy its taste and simplicity!

SERVES 2

2 pork chops
Olive oil
1 red onion, finely chopped
½ teaspoon chilli flakes (more if you want a very hot sauce!)
80–100g golden syrup
Seasoning to taste

Place the chops in the base of an oiled ovenproof dish. Preheat the NuWave oven to HI..

Place on the rack and cook for 10–12 minutes, or until the chops are almost cooked to your desired taste.

While they are cooking, fry your onion in a dash of olive oil. Add the chilli flakes. Remove from the heat and add the golden syrup. This will melt in the pan and become more fluid.

When the chops are ready, pour the sauce over them. Place back in the NuWave Oven for another 5 minutes.

Serve immediately.

Toad in the Hole

A family favourite that never fails to impress.

SERVES 2

Olive oil
2–4 sausages, ideally lean
100g plain flour
2 eggs
180ml milk
Black pepper
Sea salt
Preheat your NuWave Oven to HI.

Place a drizzle of olive oil in your ovenproof dish and brush it around all the edges.

Place the sausages in the dish and pop it on the middle rack. Cook for 10–15 minutes until the sausages start to brown and crisp.

Meanwhile, mix the flour, eggs and milk. Season well and leave to one side.

When the sausages are brown, remove from the oven and immediately pour the batter into the dish. This may sizzle a bit so be careful.

Return this to the oven and cook for another 15–20 minutes until golden and firm to touch.

Serve with mash, seasonal vegetables and gravy.

Gammon Steaks with Parsley Sauce and Mini Roasts

SERVES 2

> 400g new potatoes, washed
> Olive oil
> Garlic & Herb seasoning
> Paprika
> 20g butter
> 20g plain flour or cornflour
> 300ml milk
> Small handful freshly chopped parsley
> Black pepper
> Sea salt
> 2 Gammon Steaks
> Vegetables of your choice, if desired

Place the potatoes on an oiled baking tray. Drizzle with olive oil and season with *Garlic & Herb seasoning*. Finish with a sprinkle of paprika. Shake the tray to ensure the potatoes are evenly covered. Add more olive oil if you think they are too dry.

Set the temperature to HI.. Place the potatoes on the rack and cook for 30-40 minutes, until the potatoes are cooked and golden.

While the potatoes are roasting, make the sauce by melting the butter in a saucepan. Add the flour and using a wooden spoon stir well to form a paste.

Gradually add the milk and continue to stir over a heat. If you start to get lumps, swap the wooden spoon for a balloon whisk and whisk well. Continue to stir/whisk until the sauce starts to thicken.

Add the parsley and season to taste. Remove from heat.

Set the temperature of the NuWave Oven to HI. Move the potatoes to the rack and place the gammon steaks on the rack as you are effectively going to grill them.

Brush the steaks lightly with olive oil. Cook for

approximately 4–5 minutes each side until they are cooked to your requirements. Timing depends on size and thickness of steaks.

While they are cooking, gently reheat the sauce but do not al to boil or it may catch and burn – I would suggest a heat. If you are cooking vegetables to accompany the meal, you will need to have these ready.

Remove the potatoes and steaks from the oven and place on your dinner plates. Pour the sauce over the steaks. Serve with peas or green vegetables.

Chicken, Leek and Mushroom Filo Pie

Whenever I make a pie in the NuWave Oven, I only pop pastry on the top as sometimes NuWave Ovens can give pies an undercooked or soggy bottom unless you bake blind first. I love the texture and simplicity of using filo. No matter how haphazardly you place the filo, it always looks like you have spent hours on the dish.

SERVES 2

Olive oil
1 small leek, sliced
3–4 rashers lean bacon, roughly chopped
1 clove garlic, crushed
4 mushrooms, quartered
150–200g cooked chicken, diced
2–3 tablespoons crème fraîche or natural Greek yoghurt
100ml milk
Seasoning to taste
Pinch of tarragon
Pinch of mixed herbs
Approx 30g butter, melted
3–5 filo sheets

Note: This is just a simple recipe – ideal for using up cooked chicken from your Sunday roast!

In a sauté pan, heat a little olive oil. Add the leek, bacon, garlic and mushrooms and cook until everything starts to soften. Add the chicken and heat thoroughly.

Add the crème fraîche or yoghurt and the milk. This should give you a nice sauce for the chicken. If you want it to be runnier, you can add more milk, or if you want it to be creamier, add more crème fraîche. Season to taste and add the herbs. Transfer to a deep pie dish.

Melt the butter in a pan or you could heat it gently in the NuWave Oven, but be careful not to burn it.

Cut each filo sheet into three. Brush each piece with a little butter and screw it up roughly. Press the screwed up pastry onto the top of the pie. Continue until you have filled the top of the pie dish.

When you are ready to cook, place the dish on the rack. Turn the temperature to HI. and cook for 20–30 minutes or until golden on top.

Serve with mashed potatoes and green vegetables.

CHAPTER 4

Fish

Fish is incredibly healthy, particularly if you opt for oily fish, rich in Omega 3. The NuWave Oven is a great tool for cooking fish, especially when foil-baked in its own juices. There are quite a few recipes involving this simple way of cooking as it is not only efficient, but better nutritionally, packing in the flavors, juices and nutrients. The fish that are especially rich in Omega 3 are mackerel, trout, herring, tuna, salmon and sardines. Most of the recipes can be made with a variety of fish, so please experiment.

Foil-baked Salmon with Mango Salsa

SERVES 2

2 salmon fillets
2–4 slices of lemon
Lemon juice
Seasoning
½ ripe mango
½ ripe avocado
½ red chilli, finely chopped
2–3 spring onions, finely chopped
½ yel pepper, diced
Zest and juice of ½ lime
Generous handful of rocket, lamb's leaf, watercress or mixed leaf salad leaves
½ cucumber, diced
Small handful chopped coriander
Preheat the NuWave Oven oven to HI.

Place each salmon fillet in the center of a piece of foil. Add one or two slices of lemon on top. Finish with a squeeze of extra lemon juice and season to taste. Wrap and place on the rack. Cook for 15–20 minutes or to your own personal taste.

Meanwhile, place the salsa ingredients (all remaining ingredients apart from the salad leaves, cucumber and coriander) together in a bowl and mash/mix well.

Just prior to serving, place the salad leaves and coriander on the plates. Place the salmon on top and drizzle with salsa. Serve with the remaining half lime on the side.

Crunchy-topped Salmon

SERVES 2

> 2–3 spring onions, finely chopped
> 30g wholemeal breadcrumbs
> 20g oats
> 15g (1 tablespoon) cornflakes, crushed
> 20g parmesan, grated (optional)
> 2–3 tablespoons natural yoghurt
> Black pepper

In a bowl, mix the spring onion, breadcrumbs, oats, cornflakes and optional parmesan. Add the natural yoghurt to help bind. Season to taste.

Place the salmon fillets on a greased baking tray. Carefully spoon over the mixture to form a generous layer on top of the fillets. Press down firmly.

Place on the middle rack and set the temperature to HI.. Cook for 10–15 minutes until golden and the fish is cooked to your specification.

Serve immediately.

Creamy Smoked Haddock Pots

These are simple to make and can be prepared in advance and kept in the fridge until needed. If you don't want to serve in individual ramekin dishes, you can prepare the mixture in one larger ovenproof dish.

SERVES 2

2 smoked haddock fillets
20g butter
1 small leek, finely chopped
Black pepper
150ml milk
150g cream cheese with herbs
50g wholemeal breadcrumbs
30g parmesan cheese, grated

Place the smoked haddock fillets on a browning tray, turn the NuWave Oven on to HI. and cook for 6 minutes.

Meanwhile, melt the butter in a sauté pan. Add the chopped leek and cook until soft. Season with black pepper before adding the milk and cream cheese.

When the fish is cooked, flake off into the sauté pan.

Transfer the mixture into ramekin dishes or a larger ovenproof dish. Level off the top.

Mix the breadcrumbs and parmesan. Season with black pepper. Sprinkle this over the fish mixture.

Place the dish(es) on the rack and cook for 10 minutes at HI until golden.

Salmon and Herb Butter Parcels

SERVES 2

 1 tablespoon butter
 Small handful of fresh herbs, finely chopped
 2 salmon fillets
 ½ lemon, sliced
 Water
 Olive oil
 Black pepper
 Mix the butter and herbs to form a herb butter.
 Cut out two squares of foil, double thickness, big enough to parcel the fillets. Place the fillets on the foil and cover with a layer of herb butter, a slice or two of lemon and a dessertspoon of water. Drizzle with a dash of olive oil and season with black pepper.

 Preheat the NuWave Oven using the preheat setting or set the temperature to HI.

 Seal the foil parcels and place them on a baking tray or directly on the rack. Cook for 15–20 minutes until the fish is tender and flaking.

 Serve with new potatoes and green vegetables.

Haddock, Egg and Gruyere Bake

This is a quick and easy dish and perfect for a comforting supper.

SERVES 2

200g haddock fillets, roughly chopped
1–2 hard-boiled eggs, halved or quartered
100ml crème fraîche
75ml milk
60g Gruyere cheese, grated
1–2 teaspoons wholegrain mustard
Seasoning
1–2 tablespoons breadcrumbs
1 tablespoon oats
30g parmesan cheese, grated

In an ovenproof dish, making sure it fits in the oven, place the chopped haddock and hard-boiled eggs.

In a bowl, mix the crème fraîche, milk, grated Gruyere and mustard. Season to taste. Spoon this over the egg and haddock mixture.

Mix the breadcrumbs, oats and parmesan together, season well and sprinkle over the crème fraîche mixture.

Preheat the NuWave Oven using the preheat setting or turn on to HI. Place the dish on the rack and bake in the oven for 15–20 minutes, until the haddock is cooked.

Serve on its own for a simple supper or with salad and new potatoes.

Baked Italian-style Cod in White Wine

SERVES 2

> Olive oil
> ½ red onion, sliced
> 1 tomato, sliced
> 2 cod fillets
> 4 sundried tomatoes in oil, drained
> 4–6 basil leaves
> Seasoning to taste
> 4 tablespoons white wine

Cut out two squares of foil, double thickness, big enough to parcel the fillets. Brush the centre of each foil square with olive oil before adding a couple of slices of onion and then a couple of slices of tomato.

Lay the fish on top of the onion and tomato. Place 2 sundried tomatoes on each fillet, followed by 2 or 3 basil leaves. Season to taste.

Pull the sides of the foil up to form a bowl shape, ready to add the wine before scrunching securely. Once secure, place on a baking tray. You can leave the fish to marinate until you are ready to cook, or cook it immediately.

Place on the rack and set the NuWave Oven to HI.. Cook for 20 minutes until the fish is tender and flaking.

Serve with new potatoes and seasonal vegetables.

Note: For extra variety, why not add some pancetta as an extra layer.

Salmon and Fennel Parcels

SERVES 2

Olive oil
2 salmon fillets
½ fennel bulb, finely sliced
Seasoning to taste
4–6 tablespoons white wine or vermouth

Cut out two squares of foil, double thickness, big enough to parcel the fillets. Brush the centre of each foil square with olive oil and lay a fillet on top. Sprinkle with the sliced fennel and season to taste.

Pull the sides of the foil up to form a bowl shape, ready for the wine to be added. Scrunch securely and place on a baking tray.

You can leave the salmon to marinate until you are ready to cook it, or cook it immediately. Place on the rack and set the NuWave Oven to HI. Cook for 20 minutes until the fish is tender and flaking.

Serve with new potatoes and seasonal vegetables.

Salmon, Garlic and White Wine Parcels

This dish takes only minutes to make and can be prepared in advance.

SERVES 2

1–2 cloves of garlic, crushed
2 teaspoons honey
1–2 teaspoons wholegrain mustard
2 tablespoons white wine
Zest of 1 lemon
Butter
1 small onion, sliced into rings
2 salmon fillets
Small handful of fresh dill, finely chopped
Seasoning to taste

Put the garlic, honey, mustard, white wine and lemon zest into a bowl and combine well.

Cut out two squares of foil, double thickness, big enough to parcel the fillets. Butter the foil and add the sliced onion rings. Place the salmon over the onion.

Spread the garlic sauce over the salmon fillets, ensuring they are coated. Add a sprinkle of dill and season to taste.

Parcel up the salmon fillets, making sure the edges are sealed well.

Preheat the NuWave Oven using the preheat setting or set the temperature to HI.. Place on the rack and cook for 15–20 minutes until the fish flakes easily.

Unwrap and serve with new potatoes and green vegetables.

Baked Trout with Creamy Lemon and Dill

SERVES 2

2 rainbow trout fillets
Olive oil
Black pepper
2 cloves of garlic, sliced
½ chilli, finely chopped
½ pepper, finely chopped
Lemon juice
Dessertspoon freshly chopped dill
2–4 dessertspoons natural yoghurt

Rub the fillets with olive oil and season with black pepper.

Cut out two sheets of foil big enough to parcel up each fillet. Lay the fish on top and place the garlic, chilli and pepper on the fish.

Mix the lemon juice (to taste), dill and yoghurt together. Season to taste. Place 1–2 dessertspoons on each fillet.

Fold the foil up to form a secure parcel and place on the middle rack. Set the temperature to HI. and bake for 15–20 minutes.

Serve with new potatoes and fresh seasonal greens.

One-pot Cod

     50–75g lean, thick bacon, cut into chunks
     50g button mushrooms, halved
     1 small onion, finely chopped
     Olive oil
     2 cod fillets
     25g butter
     Sea salt
     Black pepper
     200ml white wine

Place the bacon, mushrooms and onion in a greased ovenproof dish. Don't choose a dish that is too large – it should be big enough to hold the fillets, but not so big that the ingredients become a bit lost. Drizzle sparingly with olive oil.

Butter one side of each fillet before placing them, buttered-side up, onto the bacon mixture. Season well with sea salt and black pepper.

Finally, drizzle over the white wine before covering with a double layer of tin foil, held securely.

Place the dish on the rack and cook at HI. for 20 minutes.

Uncover and cook for a further 5 minutes before serving with new potatoes and green seasonal vegetables.

Tuna and Sweetcorn Lasagne

SERVES 2

> 200g tuna (roughly 1 tin), mashed
> 2–3 spring onions, chopped
> 100g sweetcorn (tinned or frozen)
> Seasoning to taste
> Lasagne sheets
> 250ml passata
> Parmesan or other cheese for topping, grated
> Black pepper

Mix the tuna, spring onion and sweetcorn together in a bowl. Season to taste.

Add a layer of tuna mash to the bottom of a small lasagne dish, cover with a layer of lasagne sheets and top with a layer of passata. Continue this process once more, ending with a layer of passata.

Preheat the NuWave Oven oven using the preheat setting or set the temperature to HI.

Grate parmesan or other cheese over the final layer of passata and sprinkle with black pepper.

Place on the rack and cook for 30–40 minutes, until golden and the pasta sheets are cooked. If the top starts to get too dark, cover with tin foil, making sure it is secure. (The cooking time can be greatly reduced if you use fresh lasagne sheets.)

Serve with salad and garlic bread.

Simple Baked Mackerel

Simple dishes are often the best. Serve this with a green salad and new potatoes for a quick and easy supper.

SERVES 2

2 mackerel fillets

Olive oil (I use oils flavoured with garlic or chilli to add more flavour)

Sea salt

Black pepper

Lemon juice

Cover the middle rack of your NuWave Oven with foil, making sure it is secure by folding it under. Brush with oil or butter to help prevent the fish from sticking.

Place the fish onto the rack skin-side up and brush with olive oil. Season with sea salt and black pepper and a squeeze of lemon juice if preferred.

Bake at 210ºC until the skin is brown. Turn the fish over and brush again with olive oil and season. Cook for another 5 minutes.

Drizzle with lemon juice and serve.

Honeyed Salmon and Asparagus Parcels

My mum passed on this recipe, which is truly delicious and so simple. Yes it is another parcel recipe but really, why not? They are so easy to make and save on washing up – what's not to like? Try to buy asparagus when in season – the taste of fresh British asparagus is second to none.

SERVES 2

10g butter
2 tablespoons runny honey
1 tablespoon Dijon mustard
Zest of ½ lemon
Seasoning to taste
2 salmon fillets
250g fresh asparagus, trimmed

Melt the butter and mix with the honey, mustard and lemon zest. Season to taste.

Prepare two squares of doubled-up foil, big enough to parcel the fish. Place the asparagus on each square, foled by the salmon. Drizzle with the honey mixture. Seal the foil parcels securely.

Turn the NuWave Oven to HI. Place the parcels on the middle rack and cook for 20–25 minutes or until the fish flakes easily.

Serve with new potatoes and green seasonal vegetables.

Simple Foil-baked Herrings

SERVES 2

>2 herrings, filleted
>2 teaspoons butter
>Zest and juice of 1 lemon
>Sea salt
>Black pepper

Scale and wash the herrings ready to cook. Place each one on a piece of greased foil, large enough to parcel the fish.

Place a spoonful of butter onto each herring, spreading it out roughly. Add the lemon zest and a generous squeeze of lemon juice. Season with sea salt and black pepper to taste.

Wrap the foil securely and place on the rack. Turn the temperature to HI and cook for 15–20 minutes until the fish is cooked to your requirements and flakes off easily with a fork.

Serve with new potatoes and fresh seasonal salad.

Creamy Haddock Gratin

SERVES 2

>2–4 haddock fillets, depending on appetite
>1 dessertspoon butter
>1 small onion, finely sliced
>Sea salt
>Black pepper
>175g crème fraîche or Total Greek yoghurt (use double cream if you don't mind the calories!)
>100ml milk
>Zest and juice of ½ lemon
>1–2 teaspoons wholegrain mustard
>50g oats
>50g wholemeal breadcrumbs
>30g freshly grated parmesan

Wash the fish fillets before spreading a thin layer of butter on one side of each. Place them buttered-side down in a greased ovenproof dish. Cover with the onion and season with sea salt and black pepper.

In a bowl, mix the crème fraîche or yoghurt with the milk, lemon zest, juice and mustard. Pour this over the fish, spreading until covered.

In a bowl, mix the oats, breadcrumbs and parmesan. Sprinkle this evenly over the creamy mixture.

Place on the rack and turn the temperature to HI. Cook for 20 minutes until golden and bubbling and the fish is cooked to your requirements.

Serve with new potatoes and seasonal vegetables or on its own for a simple supper.

Note: For variation, you could add a thickly sliced hard-boiled egg over the onion slices, before adding the creamy mixture.

Easy Pesto Salmon

This really is a simple dish. Try to remember to marinate for at least 1 hour, but ideally 3–4 hours before cooking as this really improves the flavour.

SERVES 2

2 salmon fillets
3 tablespoons white wine or vermouth
Zest and juice of ½ lemon
Black pepper
2–3 tablespoons pesto
1 tablespoon wholemeal breadcrumbs

Place the fish fillets in a freezer bag. Add the white wine, lemon juice and zest. Season to taste with black pepper. Seal, shake well and leave in the fridge to marinate.

When ready to cook, turn the NuWave Oven to (240–250ºC) as you are going to grill the salmon.

Remove the salmon from the bag and place on a greased baking tray. Spread the pesto over the top of each fillet. Finish with a sprinkle of fresh breadcrumbs.

Place on the middle rack and cook for 10 minutes or until the fish is done to your requirements. You should be able to flake the fish with a fork.

Serve immediately.

One-pot Roasted Fish, Fennel and Red Onion

SERVES 2

2–4 white fish fillets, depending on appetite
1 small fennel bulb, sliced
1 red onion, sliced
1–2 cloves of garlic, finely sliced
1 lemon, cut into wedges
Juice of 1 lemon
Olive oil
Butter
Seasoning to taste

Season the fish fillets well and squeeze over a little lemon juice. Leave to one side until needed.

Preheat the NuWave Oven oven using the preheat setting or set the temperature to 220°C.

Place the sliced fennel, onion, garlic and lemon wedges into a roasting or baking tray, making sure it fits in your NuWave Oven.

Drizzle with olive oil and place in the oven on the rack for 15 minutes.

Place the fish fillets on top of the vegetables. Place a small knob of butter on each fillet. Drizzle the juice of 1 lemon over the dish. Season to taste and cover securely with foil. Bake for another 15–20 minutes until the fish is thoroughly cooked and flakes easily off the fork.

Remove the foil and serve with new potatoes and a fresh green salad.

Salmon, Honey and Mustard Crusts

Simple yet delicious

SERVES 2

2 salmon fillets
Juice of ½ lemon
1–2 tablespoons wholegrain mustard
1–2 tablespoons honey
1 tablespoon wholemeal breadcrumbs
1 tablespoon cornflakes, crushed (if you don't have cornflakes, use finely chopped nuts)

Squeeze the lemon juice over the salmon fillets.

Mix the mustard and honey together. In another bowl, mix the breadcrumbs and cornflakes together.

Spread the mustard coating on the fillets ensuring the tops are well coated. Then dip them into the breadcrumb mixture, again ensuring they are well coated.

Preheat the NuWave Oven oven using the preheat setting or set the temperature to HI..

Place the fillets on a baking tray on the rack. Cook for 12–15 minutes until the fillets are cooked.

Serve with a green salad and new potatoes.

Salmon Fish Cakes

SERVES 2

    200g fresh or tinned salmon
    200g potatoes, cooked and mashed
    1–2 teaspoons lemon juice
    1 teaspoon each of fresh dill and tarragon (or ½ teaspoon each of dried)
    1 egg, beaten
    Olive oil

Mix the fish, potato, lemon juice and herbs together in a bowl. Add the egg to bind.

Form the mixture into cakes, place on baking parchment and chill in the fridge for 10 minutes.

Preheat the NuWave Oven oven using the preheat setting or set the temperature to HI.

Remove the fish cakes from the fridge and brush with a light coating of olive oil.

Place on the rack either on a baking tray or a browning pan, or you can place them directly on the rack. Cook the cakes for 5–6 minutes each side, turning halfway through to ensure they are evenly cooked and browned. (You are actually grilling them at this heat.)

Serve with new potatoes and a green salad.

Mackerel and Cider Parcels

Yet another foil parcel but, really, the NuWave Oven is made for this type of recipe and they are so very easy. You can also prepare the parcels in advance, leaving them to marinate in the fridge.

SERVES 2

2 mackerel fillets (or 2 small whole mackerel, filleted)
Butter
1 small red onion, sliced
2 thick slices of lemon
2–4 tablespoons cider
Small handful of freshly chopped parsley
Black pepper
Sea salt

Wash the fillets. Cut two pieces of foil, large enough to parcel each fillet, and grease the centre of each with butter.

Place the red onion slices on each piece of foil. Place the mackerel on top, foled by a slice of lemon.

Pull the sides of the foil up as if you are ready to seal, which will prevent the cider from escaping. Then add the cider, parsley, and season with black pepper and sea salt. Close the parcel securely.

When you are ready to cook, place the parcels on the rack and set the temperature to HI.. Cook for 15–20 minutes until done to your requirements.

Serve with green salad and new potatoes.

Italian Style Tuna & Mushroom Bakes

SERVES 2

  2 large portobello or flat mushrooms
  Olive oil
  1 clove of garlic, finely crushed
  1 small red onion, finely chopped
  2 tomatoes, finely chopped
  4-5 leaves of basil, finely chopped
  75g tuna, mashed
  30-40g feta, crumbled
  Black pepper
  Sea salt
  Sprinkle of parmesan

Wash the mushrooms. Brush them with olive oil and sprinkle with a little garlic.

Place on the rack on a browning tray. Turn the temperature to HI. and cook for 8 minutes.

Meanwhile combine the remaining ingredients apart from the parmesan. Season to taste.

When the mushrooms have finished cooking, place the mixture in the centre, stuffing them well. Finish with a sprinkle of parmesan.

Place back on the rack and cook for a further 10–15 minutes until soft and golden.

Serve with green salad.

Haddock Fishcakes

SERVES 2

> 350g potatoes, cooked and mashed
> 100g haddock, skinned, boned and chopped
> 4 spring onions, finely chopped,
> 1 egg, beaten
> Sea salt
> Black pepper
> Small handful chopped parsley
> Olive oil

Cook and mash the potatoes until they are light and fluffy. Add the flaked/chopped haddock, spring onions and the egg and combine well.

Add the chopped parsley. Season to taste.

Roll into balls before flattening into cakes. Place each cake on a greased browning tray. Brush with olive oil.

When ready to cook, place on the rack and cook at HI, turning occasionally until cooked to perfection.

Serve with green salad.

Cheesy Fish Crumble

SERVES 2

225g white fish
300ml milk
1 bay leaf
Sea salt
Black pepper
Olive oil
50g butter
1 small onion, finely chopped
1 small leek, trimmed and sliced
1 small carrot, peeled and chopped into small pieces
1 large potato, peeled and cut into small pieces
80g plain flour
150ml fish or vegetable stock
½ teaspoon dried dill

Crumble topping:
50g butter
75g plain flour
50g grated parmesan cheese
½ teaspoon mustard powder

Place the fish in a pan with the milk, bay leaf and seasoning to taste. Bring to the boil and cook for 8–10 minutes until tender.

Remove the fish from the milk, keeping the milk for later. Gently flake the fish into a greased ovenproof dish.

Put a dash of olive oil and half the butter into a sauté pan. Gently cook the vegetables for 2 minutes before adding a lid. Reduce the heat to and cook gently for 10–15 minutes.

Meanwhile, melt the remaining butter in a saucepan, add the flour and cook for 1 minute, stirring continually with a wooden spoon. Add the remaining milk and stock, and continue to stir until it starts to thicken.

Remove from the heat, season to taste and add the dill.

Pour the sauce over the fish.

To make the topping, simply rub the butter and the flour together (it will look like breadcrumbs). Stir in the cheese and the mustard powder. Season to taste. Scatter this over the fish mixture.

Place on the rack and set the temperature to HI. Cook for 15–20 minutes until golden and bubbling.

Serve with green vegetables.

CHAPTER 5

Vegetarian

You don't have to be a vegetarian to enjoy vegetarian food. Nutritionally I would advise people to have at least two meat-free days a week. A diet rich in fresh, wholesome vegetables, fruit, nuts and seeds, along with oily fish is really what we should all strive for. This chapter contains some simple dishes which should appeal to all tastes. Cheese and eggs do appear frequently simply because that is what people love, but if you are watching your weight and cholesterol levels, try to cut down on the cheese consumption. There are many half fat/ fat Cheddars on the market now which work really well in most recipes, and taste-wise there is really no difference.

Goat's Cheese and Sundried Tomato Tower

Not so much a tower I suppose, but definitely an eye-catching and very, very tasty dish. This recipe takes a maximum of 15 minutes from the start of preparation until you sit down to eat. It also has the look of a very professional dish – excellent for a quick and tasty supper or reduce the quantities and make it a dinner party starter.

SERVES 2

2 portobello mushrooms (or large flat mushrooms)
Garlic-infused olive oil
100g goat's cheese
Black pepper to taste
2 generous handfuls of a selection of salad leaves (ideally rocket, watercress, spinach with lettuce leaves)
¼ cucumber, diced into
3–4 inch chunks
½ red pepper, diced
2–3 spring onions, chopped
½ green apple, diced
½ orange, peeled and sliced
8–10 cherry tomatoes, halved
25g toasted pine nuts or seeds
2 slices of ciabatta bread
4–6 sundried tomatoes (in oil, drained)
Drizzle of balsamic vinegar
Drizzle of sweet chilli sauce

Wash the mushrooms, remove the stalks and brush with the garlic-infused olive oil. Fill the cup of each mushroom with goat's cheese. Season with black pepper. Place on the rack and cook at HI for 8 minutes.

While that is cooking, place the salad leaves on two dinner plates. On top of the leaves, sprinkle the cucumber, pepper, spring onions, apple, orange slices, cherry tomatoes and pine nuts.

When the timer beeps, or if you are timing it by eye,

add the ciabatta slices to the rack and continue to cook for another 3–4 minutes.

When ready, place the ciabatta in the centre of each dinner plate. Place the mushroom over the bread, foled by 2–3 sundried tomatoes.

Finish with a drizzle of balsamic vinegar and sweet chilli sauce. Serve immediately.

Muffin Pizzas

This really is a simple, cheat dish but yummy, especially when served with a lovely bed of salad as given in the recipe opposite.

SERVES 2

1–2 muffins, sliced in half horizontally

2–4 teaspoons pasta sauce

Pizza topping of your choice, e.g. *Red onion, goat's cheese and spinach leaves Mozzarella and tomato Pepperoni Ham and pineapple*

Cheese, grated (e.g. mature Cheddar, mozzarella, parmesan)

Dried oregano

Seasoning to taste

Place the sliced muffins on your worktop and spread with the pasta sauce.

Add your choice of topping and end with a coating of grated cheese. Finish with a sprinkle of oregano and seasoning to taste.

Place on the rack and cook at HI for 8–10 minutes until golden.

Serve immediately.

Veggie Yorkshire

Yorkshire puddings are so easy to make. Stuff them with roasted vegetables and serve with roast potatoes for a delicious meal.

SERVES 2

1 small red onion, cut into wedges
2–3 cloves of garlic, halved
½ red pepper, cut into wedges
8 cherry or vine tomatoes, left whole
Olive oil
Balsamic vinegar (optional)
Sugar
Black pepper
Sea salt
Sprigs of thyme
50g plain flour
150ml milk
1 egg

In an ovenproof dish (this will also finally hold the Yorkshire mixture), place the vegetables and finish with a drizzle of olive oil, a dash of balsamic (optional) and a tiny sprinkle of sugar. Season with black pepper and sea salt and add the thyme sprigs. Place on the rack and cook for 20 minutes at HI..

While that is cooking, beat the flour, milk and egg together until you have a smooth batter. Place this in the fridge until needed.

When the vegetables are done, leave them in the oven but spread them evenly in the dish. Immediately pour the batter onto the vegetables and shut the NuWave Oven lid. Cook at HI. for 20 minutes until risen and golden.

Serve immediately.

Warm Beetroot Salad

This recipe is truly delicious.

SERVES 2

1–2 beetroots, peeled and cubed
1–2 parsnips, peeled and cubed
1 small sweet potato, peeled and cubed
Olive oil
¼ teaspoon dried oregano
Sea salt
Black pepper
Balsamic vinegar
2 handfuls of seasonal salad leaves, washed
1 small red onion, sliced (or 4–5 spring onions, sliced)
½ red pepper, sliced
50g feta or soft goat's cheese

Place the cubed root vegetables (all cut to a similar size) in a tin or browning tray. Drizzle with olive oil, ensuring the vegetables are all evenly coated. Sprinkle with oregano, sea salt, black pepper and a drizzle of balsamic.

Place on the middle rack and set the temperature to HI. Cook for 20 minutes, or until soft and sweet.

Meanwhile, place the salad leaves in your serving dishes. Add the chopped red onion (or spring onions) and the red pepper. Toss to ensure everything is evenly distributed.

When the vegetables are cooked, simply place in them in the centre of your salad, finishing with a sprinkle of feta or goat's cheese.

Serve immediately.

Cheese and Herb Soufflés

I know you are probably thinking, soufflés are not quick and easy, but really, they are. We all fear soufflés, but with practice, they really can be straightforward. Give them a try and, you know what they say, practice makes perfect.

SERVES 2

25g butter
20g plain flour
75ml milk
125g ricotta cheese
15g parmesan cheese, grated
2 eggs, separated
1 additional egg white
Handful of fresh herbs, chopped (such as parsley, thyme, chives, oregano or rosemary)

To start the soufflés, make a roux, which is a basic start to a white sauce. Melt the butter in a pan and add the flour, stirring well using a wooden spoon to avoid lumps. Add the milk and change to a balloon whisk (this helps avoid lumps). Cook until the sauce thickens and then remove from the heat.

Add the ricotta and parmesan cheese, before adding the 2 egg yolks, herbs and seasoning.

In a clean bowl (this should not have any grease on it or the egg white won't fluff up), add the 3 egg whites. Beat until the mixture forms stiff peaks. Once achieved, fold in a spoonful of the ricotta mixture as this will help loosen the egg whites and help you combine the rest of the mixture.

When you have done this, you can then add the egg whites to the rest of the cheese mixture and fold carefully. Don't over-fold or they could go flat.

Grease your soufflé dishes and pour in the mixture until it reaches the top.

Preheat the NuWave Oven - set the temperature to HI.

Place the soufflés in a deep tray, making sure it fits in your NuWave Oven. Fill the tray with hot water until it

85

reaches halfway up the soufflé dishes.

Place on the rack and cook for 20–25 minutes until the soufflés are firm, risen and golden but have a soft centre.

Serve immediately before they slump.

Italian-style Devilled Mushrooms

This is a lovely starter or snack – simple to make but tastes delicious. For extra yumminess, add some crumbled goat's cheese over the mushrooms during the last 5 minutes of baking.

SERVES 2

1–2 tablespoons sundried tomato purée
1 teaspoon wholegrain mustard
2 cloves of garlic, crushed
1 tablespoon olive oil
2 sprigs of fresh thyme, finely chopped
Sea salt
Black pepper
2–4 large mushrooms (depending on appetite)

In a bowl, mix together all the ingredients apart from the mushrooms.

Place the mushrooms on a greased baking tray and cover with the paste. Cover the tray with clingfilm and place in the fridge to marinate for at least 1 hour.

When you are ready to cook, heat the NuWave Oven to HI.. Place the tray on the rack and cook for 8–10 minutes or until the mushrooms are cooked to your satisfaction.

Serve on a bed of green salad.

Spicy Roasted Sweet Potato with Yoghurt Dressing

SERVES 2

    1 sweet potato, evenly diced
    1 red onion, quartered
    1–2 cloves of garlic, roughly chopped
    Drizzle of olive oil
    ½ chilli
    2–3cm knuckle of fresh ginger
    1 teaspoon coriander seeds
    1 teaspoon cumin seeds
    ½ teaspoon turmeric
    Seasoning
    Small handful of fresh coriander leaves, chopped
    1–2 tablespoons thick yoghurt (I prefer using a Greek yoghurt such as Total)

Turn on your NuWave Oven oven to HI..

In an ovenproof dish, add the sweet potato (making sure it is evenly diced), onion and garlic, and coat/toss well in the olive oil. Place on the rack and cook for 10 minutes.

Meanwhile, chop the chilli, grate the ginger and crush the coriander, cumin and turmeric. Mix together thoroughly. Season to taste.

Once the sweet potato has cooked for 10 minutes, lift the NuWave Oven lid and sprinkle the spices over the vegetables. Carefully toss again, ensuring it is all well covered. If necessary you can add a little more oil but it should not be soaked in oil – just lightly covered.

Turn the NuWave Oven back on to HI. and cook for another 15–20 minutes until the potato is soft.

Then remove and place in a serving dish. Add the chopped coriander leaves and serve with a dollop of yoghurt.

Baked Fennel

Fennel is a really under-rated vegetable. It has a lovely flavour and goes well with fish dishes as well as vegetarian or meat dishes. This is a very simple side dish.

SERVES 2

1–2 fennel bulbs, cut into wedges
Olive oil
1–2 cloves of garlic, chopped
Sea salt
Black pepper
Place the fennel in a pan of boiling water and simmer gently for 10 minutes. Drain and place in an oiled ovenproof dish.

Drizzle with olive oil and add the chopped garlic. Season with sea salt and black pepper.

Place on the rack and set the temperature to HI. Cook for 20–25 minutes.

Serve with a drizzle of extra virgin olive oil.

Mediterranean-style Pasta Bake

SERVES 2

150g penne pasta
Olive oil
1 small red onion, finely chopped
2 cloves of garlic, roughly chopped
1 courgette, sliced
½ red pepper, diced
200g chopped tomatoes
1–2 sprigs of thyme
Black pepper
Sea salt
Red wine (optional)
10–20g parmesan, grated

Place the dried pasta in a pan of boiling water and cook as per the manufacturer's instructions.

Meanwhile, in a sauté pan, heat a dash of olive oil and add the onion, garlic, courgette and red pepper. Cook until they start to soften before adding the chopped tomatoes and thyme. Season to taste. If you like a richer sauce you might want to add a dash or two of red wine.

Drain the pasta and add to the vegetable mixture. Combine well before placing in an ovenproof dish. Sprinkle with parmesan.

Set the NuWave Oven oven to HI.. Place the dish on the rack and cook until golden and bubbling – this should only take 5 minutes or so.

Serve immediately with crusty bread and a salad.

Goat's Cheese, Broccoli and Tomato Tart

This is a really lovely quiche-style tart and perfect for using up any leftovers. I adore the taste of goat's cheese in cooking but if you don't fancy it, why don't you opt for a strong mature cheese instead? The NuWave Oven is not the best oven for pastry bases, so I would strongly advise following the instructions and pre-baking the pastry case. This recipe will line a small flan tin.

SERVES 2

100g plain flour
50g cold butter
100g crème fraîche
70ml milk
2 eggs, 1 beaten, 1 separated
Seasoning to taste
Handful of fresh herbs (parsley, oregano or chives)
60g goat's cheese
75g broccoli, cooked
100g cherry tomatoes, halved

In a bowl, add the flour and the cold butter. Using your fingertips, rub until the butter mixes with the flour. It should look a bit like breadcrumbs. Add a little cold water until you form a firm but not too wet dough. Wrap this in clingfilm and place in the fridge to rest for half an hour.

When the pastry is ready to roll, lightly dust your work surface with flour. Press the dough into a flat circle, dusting top and bottom to ensure it does not stick. With even strokes, roll the pastry a few times then turn clockwise – this will ensure you maintain the circle for your tin. When ready, fold the end of the circle over your rolling pin and roll slightly to gather up the pastry. Unroll over the tin and press down firmly around the edges and base.

Prick with a fork before lining with parchment and covering with baking beans. (You could use dried pulses such as chickpeas or even rice if you don't have any baking beans.)

Place in the NuWave Oven on the rack. Set the temperature to HI and cook for 15 minutes.

Remove the baking beans and bake for another 5–10 minutes until cooked. Remove from the oven.

In a jug, beat the crème fraîche with the milk and 1 whole egg. Separate the remaining egg and add the yolk to the crème fraîche. Brush the pastry case with the egg white – this helps prevent the mixture making the pastry too wet. Then add the remaining egg white to the crème fraîche. Season the crème fraîche mixture with black pepper, salt and a handful of fresh herbs if you prefer.

Place the goat's cheese, broccoli and tomatoes in the pastry case. Pour the crème fraîche mixture over the vegetables.

Place back onto the rack and cook at HI. for 30 minutes or until set and golden.

Serve hot or cold.

Cheesy Egg Gratin

I used to have this when I was a child and it is surprisingly filling and comforting – a great, tasty supper. Simple to prepare, this dish can be made in advance and heated in the NuWave Oven. The cheats could buy readymade cheese sauce, or mix crème fraîche with mature cheddar and a little milk, but for me there is nothing like the taste of a fresh, traditional cheese sauce.

SERVES 2

4 eggs
10g butter
15g plain flour or cornflour
300ml milk
30–60g mature Cheddar, grated (depending on taste)
Black pepper
Sea salt
¼ teaspoon mustard (optional)
2 tomatoes, sliced
2 tablespoons oats
2 tablespoons breadcrumbs
1 tablespoon mature Cheddar or parmesan, grated

Place the eggs in boiling water and cook them for 10 minutes until they are hard-boiled. Alternatively, you could actually hard-boil the eggs in the NuWave Oven. To do this, place the eggs in the NuWave Oven egg rack and set the temperature to HI. Cook for 10 minutes or until they are ready. Take care removing the eggs from the NuWave Oven as they can be very hot.

While the eggs are cooking, start to prepare the cheese sauce. In a heavy-based saucepan on a heat, melt the butter and then add the flour. Using a wooden spoon, mix the butter and flour to form a paste-like dough. Add a little milk at a time and continue to stir. If lumps begin to develop in the sauce, switch to a balloon whisk and beat well. This will ensure a lovely smooth sauce. Add the cheese and continue to stir until it has melted and you are left with a glossy sauce.

Once thickened, season with black pepper and sea salt and add the mustard.

Shell the hard-boiled eggs and halve them. Place in the bottom of an ovenproof dish. Pour the cheese on top and add the tomato slices.

Mix the oats, breadcrumbs and tablespoon of cheese together, season and sprinkle this over the tomatoes.

Place on the rack and set the temperature to HI. Cook until golden and bubbling – this should only take 5–8 minutes. If you are cooking this as a preprepared dish from cold, reduce the temperature to HI. and cook for 15 minutes.

Tomato and Mozzarella Puff Tarts

Puff pastry is the busy cook's best friend. You can create your own toppings but this is a simple favourite to help get you started.

SERVES 2

¼ pack of readymade puff pastry
2 teaspoons sundried tomato paste
½ pack of mozzarella Handful of basil leaves
4–5 cherry tomatoes
Seasoning to taste
Extra basil leaves to garnish

Roll out the pastry to a 2–3mm thickness. Cut into 2–3 squares. Carefully score around the edge of each square with a knife, 1cm from the edge of the pastry – do not cut the pastry, just make a slight indent.

Preheat the NuWave Oven oven using the preheat setting or turn on to HI.

In the middle of each square add a teaspoon of sundried tomato paste and spread evenly within the scored line. Place pieces of mozzarella and a few leaves of basil inside the scored line. Add a few cherry tomatoes, halved or whole, depending on your preference. Season to taste.

Place on the rack and bake in the oven for about 15 minutes until the pastry is golden. If the tarts start to brown before the base is cooked, transfer to the rack for a few more minutes.

Before serving, add a garnish of basil leaves.

Simple Mushroom Bake

SERVES 2

> 2 slices of white bread (crusts removed)
> Butter
> 100g of sliced mushrooms (a mixture of oyster and chestnut is good)
> 1 clove of garlic, crushed
> ½ teaspoon mustard
> 150ml vegetable stock
> Black pepper
> Sea salt
> Small handful of freshly chopped parsley
> 1 tablespoon crème fraîche
> Snipped chives to garnish

Flatten the bread slices with a rolling pin and roll them out as thinly as you can. Place each piece of bread into a 10cm (4in) tartlet tin, leaving the bread extending up the sides of the tin. Place on the rack of your NuWave Oven and set the temperature to HI. Bake for 8–10 minutes, then remove and place to one side.

In a sauté pan, melt a small knob of butter. Add the mushrooms and garlic and cook until the mushrooms start to soften. Remove the mushrooms from the pan with a slotted spoon and transfer to a heatproof dish. Cover with a lid or foil and place into the oven to keep warm – set the temperature to 120°C.

Add the mustard and stock to the pan. Reduce the juices in the pan, by cooking for 2–3 minutes, until the sauce thickens.

Remove from the heat. Season and add the chopped parsley and crème fraîche. Combine well.

Remove the mushrooms from the oven. Place the bread cases on plates and share the mushroom mixture between them, spoon over the sauce and garnish with the chopped chives.

Serve immediately with a large green salad.

Vegetable Mornay Bake

A family favorite, suitable as a main meal or even a side dish. Have a look in your local supermarket as they often sell broccoli and caulifer florets in a bag which is enough for two people – cheaper than buying whole heads and wasting them.

SERVES 2

1 carrot
1 small leek
½ small head of broccoli
½ small cauliflower
10g butter
10g plain flour or cornflour
250–300ml milk
1 tablespoon nutritional yeast flakes (optional)
60g mature cheese, grated
¼ teaspoon mustard (optional)
Black pepper
1 tablespoon oats
1 tablespoon home-prepared wholemeal breadcrumbs
20g parmesan cheese

Chop the carrot into sticks, slice the leek and cut the broccoli and caulifer into manageable florets. Place in a steamer and cook until the caulifer is tender but not soft.

Meanwhile, make the sauce. Melt the butter gently in a saucepan on a heat (not !). Add the flour or cornflour and stir well with a wooden spoon. Add the milk a little at a time, continuing to stir to avoid lumps.

Switch now to a balloon whisk. Continue to stir over a heat until the sauce begins to thicken. The balloon whisk will also help to eradicate any lumps that may have formed. Add more milk as necessary to get the desired thickness. The sauce should be the thickness of custard.

If you are using nutritional yeast flakes, add these before the grated cheese as they will reduce the amount of cheese you will need – taste as you go! Add the cheese and mustard and stir well. Season with black pepper.

When the vegetables are ready, transfer them to an ovenproof dish. Pour on the cheese sauce, ensuring all the vegetables are covered.

Mix the oats, breadcrumbs and parmesan together thoroughly. Scatter over the cheese sauce.

Preheat the NuWave Oven using the preheat setting or set the temperature to HI.

Place the mornay on the rack. Cook for 15–20 minutes until the top is golden and crispy.

Spinach and Ricotta Lasagne

I have had so many compliments about this recipe which appears in other books I have written that I just had to include it here also, altered to serve two. We enjoy this dish at least twice a month. It has some great flavors, so even if you aren't vegetarian give it a try as I am sure it will impress. Unlike most lasagne recipes, this one takes just minutes to prepare. I recommend using *Seeds of Change Cherry Tomato, Basil and Parmesan Pasta Sauce* – it has an authentic homemade taste and look.

SERVES 2

½ onion, finely chopped
½ pot of ricotta
50g mature Cheddar, grated
75g fresh spinach leaves (baby spinach is best)
Grated nutmeg
Black pepper to taste
Lasagne sheets
1 small jar of pasta sauce
Grated parmesan or other cheese for topping

Place the onion, ricotta and Cheddar in a bowl and mix well. Add the spinach leaves. (Placing the spinach in a colander and running it under a hot tap for a few seconds softens the leaves and makes the mixing easier.)

Once mixed, add some grated nutmeg and season with black pepper.

Place a thin layer of ricotta mixture in the bottom of a lasagne dish, foled by a layer of lasagne sheets. (If you use fresh lasagne sheets, the cooking time can be halved. Alternatively, you could boil the dried lasagne sheets for a few minutes before using.) Top with a thin layer of pasta sauce. Continue with a layer of ricotta, then lasagne, and finally the remaining pasta sauce. Add approximately 30ml of water to the empty jar, rinse the jar and pour the water over the top of the lasagne.

Grate some parmesan or other cheese onto the lasagne and season.

Preheat the NuWave Oven by selecting HI.

Place the lasagne on the rack and cook for 35–45 minutes. If the top starts to get too dark, cover with tin foil, making sure it is secure.

Serve with potato wedges and salad – delicious!

Roasted Mixed Vegetables with Garlic Dip

A really simple dish – perfect for friends to dig in and enjoy!

SERVES 2

2–3 cloves of garlic, crushed
1 onion, cut into thick wedges
2 small carrots, peeled and cut into large batons
1 small parsnip, peeled and cut into large batons
2 potatoes, peeled and quartered
¼–½ fennel bulb, sliced thickly
2–3 sprigs of thyme
Sea salt
Black pepper
Olive oil
125g garlic/herb cream cheese
2 tablespoons milk
Zest of ½ lemon

Place all vegetables and herbs into an ovenproof dish. Season with salt and pepper. Drizzle with olive oil and mix lightly, ensuring everything is evenly distributed.

Set the NuWave Oven to HI.. Place the dish on the rack and bake for 30–40 minutes or until the vegetables are golden and roasted.

While that is cooking, melt the cream cheese, milk and lemon zest in a pan. Season to taste.

Place the cooked vegetables onto a serving dish. Pour the sauce into ramekin dishes and place by the dish as a dip. Serve immediately.

Stuffed Tomatoes

You could use any leftover cooked rice for this dish instead of making fresh rice.

SERVES 2

50g rice
300ml vegetable stock
Olive oil
1 small onion, finely chopped
1 clove of garlic, crushed
½ green or yel pepper, deseeded and chopped
½ red chilli, deseeded and finely chopped
25g mushrooms, finely chopped
1 teaspoon oregano
Sea salt
Black pepper
1 small egg, beaten
2 large ripe beef tomatoes
1 teaspoon caster sugar

Place the rice into a saucepan with the stock and bring to the boil. Simmer until tender. Drain and place to one side.

Place some olive oil in a small pan and fry the onion, garlic, pepper, chilli and mushrooms for 2 minutes.

Add to the rice with the oregano and seasoning and combine well. Remove from the heat. Stir in the beaten egg and mix again.

Slice the tops off the tomatoes, but don't discard them. Scoop out the flesh and add this to the rice mixture.

Sprinkle the sugar into the base of each tomato before filling with the rice mixture.

Place the tomatoes on a greased baking tray. Add the

tomato lids and brush with a little oil (I use garlic oil for this).

Place on the rack and cook at HI. for 20 minutes.

Serve immediately with fresh crusty bread and salad.

Roasted Vegetable Curry

I adore curries and roasted vegetables so why not put the two together. It creates a very simple curry dish that tastes fantastic.

SERVES 2–3

1 red onion, cut into wedges
1 sweet potato, thickly diced
1 potato, thickly diced
½ small butternut squash, unpeeled and cut into 2cmthick chunks or wedges
1 carrot, thickly sliced
Olive oil
Seasoning
Paprika
½ teaspoon coriander seeds
½ teaspoon cumin seeds
½ red chilli
2 cloves garlic
½in knuckle of ginger
1 teaspoon turmeric
1 teaspoon garam masala
Small handful of coriander leaves
3–4 spring onions
200–300ml water
75–150ml fat coconut milk
1–2 tablespoons Greek yoghurt
2 tomatoes, cut into wedges
½ red pepper, deseeded and thickly sliced
Extra coriander leaves to garnish
Preheat the NuWave Oven to HI.

Prepare your vegetables. Place the red onion, potatoes, butternut squash and carrot in an ovenproof dish (making sure it fits in your NuWave Oven). Drizzle with olive oil and a sprinkle of seasoning and paprika and toss until combined, ensuring the vegetables are evenly coated in oil. Place the vegetables on the rack and cook for 20 minutes.

Meanwhile, place the coriander seeds and cumin seeds in a dry, large sauté pan and heat gently for 1–2 minutes. When the fragrance starts to break through, crush the warmed seeds in a pestle and mortar and combine. Leave the sauté pan to one side, as you will need this in a moment.

In your liquidiser, add the spices, chilli, garlic, ginger, turmeric, garam masala, coriander leaves, spring onions and seasoning. Combine well. Add olive oil until a runnier paste forms.

Place this paste into the sauté pan and heat gently. Add 200ml of water and combine, while bringing up to the boil. Once boiling, turn off the heat. Finally, add the coconut milk and Greek yoghurt to the curry paste in the sauté pan. Combine well. Leave to one side.

By now your vegetables should be almost ready for the next stage. Once the 15-minute timer beeps, add the tomatoes and red pepper. Combine well and add a drizzle more oil if necessary. Return to the oven for another 15 minutes.

Remove the vegetables from the NuWave Oven. Add these to your paste in the sauté pan. Add more water if you want a runnier curry, bearing in mind that some liquid will evaporate during the cooking. Cook for another 5–10 minutes until the vegetables are roasted to your taste.

Sprinkle with coriander leaves. Serve with fluffy, fragrant rice, yoghurt and chutney.

S-Cook Tuscan-style Tomato and Beans

I love this dish. I tend to make a large batch and it lasts me a few meals – a lovely lunch with crusty bread, add pasta and you have a more filling meal, or simply on its own with a handful of crumbled feta. Delicious!

SERVES 2

> 1 small red onion, cut into thick slices
> 3-4 tomatoes, cut into thick wedges
> ½ red pepper, deseeded and cut into thick wedges
> 2 cloves of garlic, roughly chopped
> Olive oil
> Balsamic vinegar
> Sea salt
> Sugar
> Black pepper
> 1-2 sprigs of thyme
> 1 200g tin of cannellini beans
> 75ml red wine

In an ovenproof dish, add the onion, tomatoes, chopped pepper and garlic. Make the vegetables chunky but small enough to eat. Drizzle over some olive oil and a dash of balsamic vinegar. Finish with a sprinkle of sea salt, black pepper and a little sugar to help sweeten.

Add the thyme sprigs and combine well, ensuring it is all well distributed and coated in the oil.

Place on the rack and turn the temperature to HI.. Cook for 20 minutes until the mixture starts to soften. You will be surprised how much liquid comes out of this.

Remove from the oven. Stir in the cannellini beans and add the wine. Place back in the oven for another 10 minutes until thoroughly cooked and the beans are warmed through.

Serve with crusty bread, add pasta to have a more filling meal, or simply on its own with a handful of crumbled feta.

Caulifer and Broccoli Cheese Gratin

SERVES 2

½ small head of caulifer
½ small head of broccoli or bag combining both.
20g butter
15g plain flour or cornflour
200ml milk
50g mature Cheddar, grated
¼ teaspoon mustard
Seasoning to taste
60g wholemeal breadcrumbs
30g oats
1 carrot, grated
20g Cheddar or parmesan, grated

Note: You can often buy broccoli and caulifer heads already bagged in the supermarket. It is more expensive than buying large heads but does avoid wastage.

Cut your caulifer and broccoli into equal-sized florets. Steam or boil these until they are only just soft – they should still have a bite and a little hardness to them – you certainly don't want a soggy mash!

Meanwhile place butter in a saucepan and melt gently on heat (not !). Add flour or cornflour and stir well with a wooden spoon. Add a little milk at a time, continuing to stir to avoid lumps.

Switch now to a balloon whisk. Continue to stir over a heat until sauce begins to thicken. The balloon whisk will also help eradicate any lumps that may have materialized. Add more milk as necessary to get desired thickness. It should be the thickness of custard.

Add the 50g of grated Cheddar cheese, mustard and

season with black pepper. Keep stirring until the cheese has melted. Taste to see if you need more cheese or seasoning.

Place the cooked caulifer and broccoli in your ovenproof dish. Pour over the cheese sauce.

In a bowl, mix the breadcrumbs, oats, carrot and Cheddar cheese or parmesan together. Season to taste.

Place this over the caulifer cheese mixture.

Place on the rack and cook at HI. for 20 minutes until golden.

Eggy Pizza

This is a really yummy and very easy recipe. I saw Nigella making something similar and I wondered if it could be adapted to work in the NuWave Oven. Yes it can and it is a really big favorite of my youngest son. You can, of course, choose whatever topping and filling ingredients you wish, but I find this works wonderfully.

SERVES 2

150g plain flour
2 eggs
150ml milk
125–150g mature Cheddar, grated
½ small onion, finely chopped
6–8 sundried tomatoes (drained from oil), chopped
1–2 teaspoons fresh oregano
Seasoning to taste
2–3 tablespoons thick, good quality pasta sauce
1 tomato, thinly sliced
Preheat the NuWave Oven to HI.

Place the flour into a mixing bowl. Beat the eggs and the milk together and pour onto the flour. Mix well. Add two-thirds of the grated cheese, along with the onion, sundried tomatoes and half the oregano. Season to taste.

Pour this into a greased baking dish or tray – I use a Victoria sponge tin but you can use a Pyrex dish or anything with sides (making sure it fits in your NuWave Oven). Place on the rack and cook for 20 minutes.

Then spread the top of the omelette/pizza with your pasta sauce. Finish with the remaining cheese and oregano, and the slices of tomato. You could add anything else – pepperoni, goat's cheese instead of Cheddar, peppers, mushrooms, etc.

Bake again for another 10 minutes before serving with a salad. A great supper!

CHAPTER 6

Desserts

The dessert is really is my favorite part of a meal, and yes, my waistline will vouch for that! This chapter contains traditional family favourites – just because you are only cooking for 1 or 2, does not mean you should go without a delicious pudding! If you want to watch your calories, substitute cream with fat crème fraîche or thick, Greek yoghurt.

Simple Bread and Butter Pudding

A delicious pudding that just screams comfort!

SERVES 2

3–4 slices of white bread (ideally slightly stale)
Butter
30g sugar
30g dried fruit (raisins, sultanas or currants)
300ml full fat milk
1 egg
½ teaspoon vanilla extract

Butter the slices of bread and place them in an ovenproof dish, layering with a sprinkle of sugar and dried fruit.

Once you have built up your layers, mix the milk and egg together. Pour this over the bread and leave it to be absorbed for at least 20 minutes.

When you are ready to cook, place on the rack and set the temperature to HI. Cook for 20–30 minutes until golden.

Note: I am a cinnamon addict so I always add a sprinkle of cinnamon between the layers.

Honey Roasted Plums with Almonds

It is not just vegetables that can be roasted – these plums are delicious when s cooked – and they are perfect for the NuWave Oven.

SERVES 2

4–6 plums, stones removed
Sugar
1–2 tablespoons liqueur, e.g. amaretto or Cointreau (optional)
Runny honey
Cinnamon powder
Sliced almonds
Preheat the NuWave Oven oven using the preheat setting or set the temperature to HI.

Wash the plums. While they are still wet, roll them in sugar and place on a greased/buttered baking tray or ovenproof dish. Add 1–2 tablespoons of water or, if you are feeling a bit naughty, some liqueur. Place on the rack and cook for 10 minutes.

Drizzle over 1–2 tablespoons of runny honey and sprinkle with some cinnamon powder and almonds. Then cook again for another 10–15 minutes until the plums are cooked.

Serve with custard, crème fraîche or ice-cream.

Lemon Saucy Pudding

SERVES 2–3

25g butter
60g sugar
Juice and zest of 1 large lemon
2 eggs, separated
1 teaspoon vanilla essence or paste
30g plain flour
150ml milk

Beat the butter and sugar together until creamy.

Add the lemon juice and zest, egg yolks and vanilla. Beat well before adding the flour and milk. This will form quite a runny batter. Give it a thorough stir to make sure there is nothing left around the side of the bowl.

Meanwhile, in a clean bowl, beat the egg whites until they form soft peaks. Fold this into the batter gently.

Line your baking dish with butter. I use a Pyrex baking dish but you could use individual ramekin dishes (see be). Pour in the mixture.

Fill the bottom of your NuWave Oven oven with hot water up to approximately 3cm (1in). Place the baking tray in the water to create a *bain marie*. If you prefer and have room, you can place a baking tray filled with water on the er rack and add small ramekin dishes filled with the mixture.

Turn the NuWave Oven to HI. and cook for 30–35 minutes (20–30 minutes for individual ramekin dishes). The pudding should have a golden sponge topping which is firm to the touch.

When you serve the pudding, you will notice that the bottom half is a gooey lemon sauce and the top should be a lovely light sponge. Serve with crème fraîche or Greek yoghurt.

Baked Jam Sponge Pudding

These old-fashioned puddings are making a welcome comeback. Go on, enjoy!

SERVES 2

50g butter
50g sugar
1 large egg
50g self-raising flour
1 tablespoon milk
½ teaspoon vanilla extract
1–2 tablespoons raspberry jam

Beat the butter and sugar together until light and fluffy. Gradually add the egg.

Sift the flour into the bowl and stir well, adding the milk and vanilla extract until a lovely batter is formed.

Butter a 600ml (1 pint) ovenproof bowl or small ovenproof dish. Place the jam in the base before adding the sponge mixture.

Preheat your NuWave Oven oven using the preheat setting or set the temperature to HI.

Place the bowl on the rack. Cook for 30 minutes until golden and firm to the touch. The sponge should be coming away slightly from the edges and should spring back when pressed. If in doubt, place a skewer or sharp knife into the centre of the pudding. If it comes out clean the pudding is done. If wet, place back in the oven and test again at 5 minute intervals.

Serve with homemade custard.

Gooey Chocolate Puddings

These are baked in little ramekin dishes and turned out immediately – they will droop and ooze out chocolate when punctured with a spoon, but that is the general appeal. Serve with a dollop of crème fraîche and a few fresh raspberries for the perfect indulgent pud!

SERVES 2

175g dark chocolate
30g butter
75g sugar
2 eggs
1 teaspoon vanilla extract
1 teaspoon chocolate extract (optional)
30g plain flour, sifted
Icing sugar

Melt the chocolate using a *bain marie* or a bowl over a saucepan of hot water (don't let the bottom of the bowl touch the water). Once melted, leave to one side.

Meanwhile, combine the butter and sugar until light and fluffy. Add the eggs, vanilla and chocolate extract. Combine well before folding in the sifted flour. Finally add the melted chocolate and combine well.

Preheat the NuWave Oven to HI..

Thoroughly grease the ramekin dishes and then dust with flour. Pour in the mixture and place on the rack. Cook for 12–15 minutes.

Turn onto a serving plate, sprinkle with icing sugar and serve with a dollop of crème fraîche and some fresh raspberries – delicious!

Apricot and Pecan Crumble

This is delicious and so simple. Dried fruit is great to have in the store cupboard and in this recipe you can use all dried fruit, or you can add some tinned peaches.

SERVES 2

>75g dried apricots, halved
>Zest and juice of 1 orange
>1 tablespoon marmalade
>1 tablespoon butter
>40g plain flour
>40g oats
>30g brown sugar
>25g pecan nuts

Place the apricots in a saucepan and pour over hot water until they are just covered. Leave to rest for 3–4 hours.

When they are ready, add the orange zest and juice and the marmalade. If the water has evaporated, add a little more, enough to moisten the apricots and to give a saucetype consistency to the fruit mixture.

Bring to the boil and cook for 20 minutes, making sure the water does not evaporate (add more if needed). Place the fruit into an ovenproof dish.

In a bowl, mix the butter into the flour until it forms a texture similar to breadcrumbs. Add the oats, sugar and pecan nuts and combine well. Place this over the apricots.

Place on the rack and cook for 15–20 minutes at HI.

Serve with a dollop of cream, ice-cream or crème fraîche.

Rhubarb and Strawberry Crumble

I love this combination. It is ideal for those strawberries that lack flavour or need using up, as they transform into yumminess when you cook them.

SERVES 2

500g rhubarb, cut into chunks
Handful of strawberries, whole or halved
30g sugar
30g butter
60g plain flour
30g oats
30g sugar

Place the rhubarb in a saucepan with a drizzle of water. Cook sly on a heat until it starts to soften. You want the rhubarb soft but not completely mushy.

Add the strawberries and stir in the sugar. Remove from the heat and pour into an ovenproof dish.

Meanwhile, in a bowl, rub the butter into the flour until it resembles breadcrumbs. Add the oats and sugar. Cover the fruit with this crumble mixture and press down gently with the back of a spoon.

Place on the rack and cook at HI. for 15–20 minutes.

Serve with a dollop of cream, crème fraîche or ice-cream.

Rich Semolina Pudding

I adore these old-fashioned puddings. This is simple to make and gives a comforting hug on a winter's evening.

SERVES 2

350ml milk
30g semolina
30g caster sugar
Zest of ½ orange
1 egg yolk
30g sultanas
Nutmeg
Brown sugar

Place the milk in a saucepan and heat until very hot. Then add the semolina and sugar, and bring to the boil, stirring constantly. The semolina will start to thicken. Don't allow it to stick or burn.

Remove from the heat and add the orange zest, egg yolk and sultanas.

Pour into an ovenproof dish. Sprinkle with a little nutmeg, brown sugar and extra orange zest. Place on the rack and cook at HI. for 10–15 minutes.

Serve immediately.

Marmalade and Apricot Bread and Butter Pudding

For chocolate addicts, add a handful of plain chocolate chips between each layer.

SERVES 2

2–4 slices of white bread (ideally stale)
Butter
1–2 tablespoons marmalade
60g apricots
1 tablespoon brown sugar
2 eggs
30g caster sugar
300ml full fat milk
Zest of 1 orange

Butter the bread on both sides, foled by the marmalade. Place the slices of bread into an ovenproof dish, so that they are slightly overlapping. While you are doing this, sprinkle chopped apricots and brown sugar between each slice.

Mix the eggs, caster sugar, milk and orange zest together. Pour over the bread. Push the bread down into the mixture to ensure it is mostly covered. Leave to stand for 10 minutes.

When ready to cook, place on the rack and set the temperature to HI. Cook for 30 minutes or until set.

Serve immediately.

Raspberry Healthy Brûlée

This is a really yummy dessert that takes just minutes to prepare. I tend to always have frozen raspberries in my freezer and yoghurt and crème fraîche in my fridge. This dessert looks and tastes far more impressive than it really is and the good news is that it is actually quite healthy!

SERVES 2–3

100g frozen raspberries (or fresh)
150–200g Greek yoghurt (I use Total 0% fat)
2 tablespoons fat crème fraîche
½ teaspoon vanilla paste
1–2 tablespoons brown sugar

Note: You can experiment by using blueberries or summer fruits instead of the raspberries.

If you are using frozen raspberries, place them on your serving dish and put it on the rack in the NuWave Oven oven. Turn to the Thaw setting for 10 minutes.

Meanwhile, mix the yoghurt and crème fraîche together in a bowl. Once combined, add the vanilla paste and stir well.

Remove the raspberries from the NuWave Oven. I tend to serve this in one serving dish but you could use individual serving dishes, though make sure they are heatproof. I keep the raspberries in the dish I thawed them in as it is heatproof. If you are using a different dish, or ramekin dishes, place the raspberries at the bottom.

Spoon over the yoghurt mixture. Then sprinkle brown sugar – enough to form a generous layer to make the crème brûlée effect.

Place back in the NuWave Oven on the rack. Turn to the est setting (usually 250°C) for 3–4 minutes, aling the brown sugar to start melting and caramelizing. The beauty of the NuWave Oven is that it enables you to see this cooking, therefore avoiding burning.

Serve and enjoy!

Queen of Puddings

My mom used to make this for us when we were children. Comforting puddings are making a well-earned revival; they are so much nicer than shop-bought, processed puddings.

SERVES 2-3

45g white bread, cubed
25g sugar
200ml milk
½ teaspoon vanilla extract or paste
25g butter
1 egg, separated
1-2 tablespoons jam (I use raspberry but feel free to use whatever you prefer)
25g caster sugar
Grease an ovenproof dish.

Place the cubed bread in a bowl and sprinkle with sugar.

In a saucepan, heat the milk, vanilla extract and butter to almost boiling point and then pour over the bread and sugar mixture. Al to cool. Then add the egg yolk and whisk until smooth. Pour this into the greased ovenproof dish.

Preheat your NuWave Oven using the preheat setting or turn the temperature to HI. Place the dish on the rack and cook for 30-35 minutes until set.

While this is cooking, beat the egg white until it forms soft peaks, gradually adding half of the caster sugar.

Melt the jam on a heat as you don't want to burn it. Spread the jam over the set mixture. Top this with your whisked egg white. Sprinkle with the remaining caster sugar.

Place back in the oven and cook for another 8-10 minutes until golden.

Apple, Chocolate and Hazelnut Crumble

This is a seriously impressive crumble, especially when you soak the sultanas as this really does make the dessert. If you are adverse to using alcohol, you could opt for orange juice.

SERVES 2

40g sultanas
3 tablespoons masala, dark rum or orange juice
100g plain flour
50g butter
30g oats
40g hazelnuts, finely chopped
30g brown sugar
25g chocolate chips
2–3 cooking apples (depending on size), sliced or diced
1 tablespoon granulated sugar

Place the sultanas in a bowl and add the alcohol or juice. Leave them to soak while you continue with the rest of the recipe.

In a large bowl, add the flour. Rub in the butter until it forms a texture similar to breadcrumbs. Add the oats, hazeluts, brown sugar and chocolate chips and combine well. Leave to one side.

Place the apples in a heavy-based saucepan. Heat gently with approximately 1–2 tablespoons of water. Al them to cook sly until they are just starting to get soft but still hold their shape. You don't want it to be mushy or puréed. Stir in the granulated sugar and soaked sultanas including any leftover juice.

Place the apple mixture in the base of an ovenproof dish. Cover with the crumble mixture and press down gently. If you want, you could add a sprinkle of brown sugar to the top of the crumble and finish with a sprinkle of hazelnuts.

Place on the rack and set the temperature to HI. Cook the crumble for 20–25 minutes.

Serve with custard, cream, ice-cream or crème fraîche.

Baked Apricot and Bananas with Dark Chocolate Sauce

SERVES 2

2 bananas

3 fresh whole apricots, halved, or one small tin of apricot halves

Drizzle of runny honey

30–40g dark chocolate, melted

10g (1 dessertspoon) butter

15g (1 tablespoon) golden syrup

Place the bananas, still in their skins, on one half of the baking tray. On the other half, add the apricot halves. Drizzle the apricots with honey.

Place the baking tray on the rack of your NuWave Oven and cook at HI until the banana skin goes black and the apricots golden (this should take no more than 10 minutes). Remove the banana skins.

Meanwhile, in a bowl placed over boiling water, melt the chocolate with the butter and the golden syrup. Then pour this over the baked bananas and apricots. Delicious!

Blackberry and Apple Upside-down Cake

SERVES 2

> 20g butter
> 20–30g golden syrup
> 1–2 Bramley cooking apples, peeled, sliced or chopped
> Small handful of blackberries
> 110g butter
> 110g sugar
> 2 eggs
> 130g self-raising flour, sifted
> ½–1 teaspoon vanilla extract
> Ground cinnamon
> Icing sugar
> *Note:* You will need to find a small cake tin – ideally

about 15cm (6in) and springform.

In a saucepan, heat the 20g butter and golden syrup until melted together.

In the base of your lined springform tin, place the sliced apples in a lovely fanned out pattern. I normally place the slices around the edges in a circle and then fill in the central gaps. Place some blackberries in any gaps.

Pour the melted syrup mixture over the apple and blackberries. Leave to stand.

Using your food mixer, beat the butter and 110g sugar until it becomes light and fluffy. Gradually add the eggs before folding in the sifted flour. Once mixed, add the vanilla and any remaining chunks of apple and blackberries. Cinnamon lovers could add a sprinkle of ground cinnamon.

Carefully pour the mixture over the apple base. Gently level out the cake mixture without disturbing the apple layer be.

Place this on the rack and set the temperature to HI.

Cook for 20–25 minutes or until the mixture is firm to the touch and an inserted cake skewer comes out clean.

Remove the cake from the oven and leave for a few

minutes, before turning out onto a heatproof dish. (Simply place the new dish on the top of the cake tin, face down, and flip over. The cake will then be bottom-side up on your new dish.) Sprinkle with icing sugar and serve hot or cold.

Baked Banana Apples with Ricotta Cream

I discovered this recipe in an 1970s good housekeeping book and thought it looked quite fun. I have adapted it slightly to suit tastes but it is perfect for the NuWave Oven. Serve with this delicious ricotta cream for some extra indulgence.

SERVES 2

2 cooking apples, cored
1–2 soft bananas, mashed
¼ teaspoon nutmeg
½ teaspoon cinnamon
1 teaspoon lemon juice
1 tablespoons brown sugar
60g ricotta
30ml Greek yoghurt
½ teaspoon cinnamon
½ teaspoon vanilla extract
1 dessertspoon clear runny honey

Place the cored apples on a greased or lined baking tray.

In a bowl, mix the banana, nutmeg, cinnamon, lemon juice and sugar together. Fill the cores of the apples with the banana mixture.

Place the apples on the rack and set the temperature to HI.

Cook for 30–40 minutes until the apples are tender.

While the apples are cooking mix the ricotta and yoghurt with vanilla, honey and cinnamon.

Remove the apples from the oven, place on your serving dish, with a generous dollop of the ricotta cream.

Cheat's Treacle Tart

If you love treacle tart, why not try this simple recipe. Using pre-baked pastry cases saves time and avoids soggy-bottom pastry! This recipe is perfect for the small pastry case found in supermarkets (approx. 6–7 inch diameter)

SERVES 2

180g golden syrup
15g (1 tablespoon) butter
25g double cream, (optional)
1 egg, beaten
50–75g breadcrumbs

In a saucepan, gently heat the golden syrup until it becomes runny. Add the butter and stir well. Add the cream (if using), and the beaten egg and combine well.

Add the breadcrumbs and stir well. You want a fluid consistency, not thick and lumpy, but with enough texture to give the golden syrup body.

Pour this into your pastry case.

Place on the rack and cook at 160°C for 30 minutes. If you need more time, turn the temperature down to 150°C and cook at 5-minute intervals, checking as you go to avoid burning. The pie should be firm and golden.

Serve with a dollop of cream, crème fraîche or natural yoghurt.

Apple Pie

Who doesn't like this family favourite? This recipe only uses a top for the pie as I find sometimes the bottom pastry can be a bit doughy – however, if you want to add a bottom, simply add a lining of pastry, baking it blind (bake with a layer of greaseproof paper and baking beans or pulses) for 10–15 minutes before adding the apple and the top. To ensure a non-soggy base you could brush the pastry bottom, once cooked, with egg-white or sprinkle with semolina.

SERVES 2

2-3 cooking apples, peeled, cored and chopped (Bramleys preferably)
1–2 dessertspoons of sugar, depending on taste
1 teaspoon ground cinnamon (optional)
1 handful of sultanas (optional)
¼ pack ready-made puff or sweet shortcrust pastry
1 egg, or a little milk to brush

Peel, core and chop the cooking apples. Place them in a saucepan with 1–2 dessert-spoons of water. Sprinkle with the sugar, cinnamon and sultanas. Cook sly so the apples just start to soften – you don't want them too soggy.

Once ready, place the apples in the deep ovenproof dish. Roll out your pastry to the required thickness – I would opt for approximately 3mm.

Brush the edge of the ovenproof dish with egg or milk. Carefully cut a strip off the edge of your rolled pastry, wide enough to cover the edge/lip of your ovenproof dish.

Carefully place this over the edge of the dish. Push down to secure. Brush again with egg or milk.

Using the edge of your rolling pin, roll up the edge of the pastry as this makes it easier to handle. Unroll onto the ovenproof dish. Push down at the edges to secure.

Go around the edges of the pastry with your finger-tips making a crimping motion, making sure it is secure. Cut off excess pastry.

Using a sharp knife, make two small slits in the top of the pastry to al the air to escape. Brush with egg or milk and sprinkle with a little sugar.

Place on the middle rack and set the temperature to HI. Cook for 20–25 minutes until the pastry is golden.

Serve with custard or a dollop of cream or ice-cream.

Apple Nut Crunch

I love simple puddings that don't require too much fiddling around but still give you a nice comforting dessert.

SERVES 2

250g cooking apples, peeled, cored and sliced
1 tablespoon brown sugar
2 wedges of lemon
½ teaspoon cinnamon (optional)
40g honey-nut cornflakes (can use ordinary cornflakes if you prefer)
1 dessertspoon butter

Place the apple slices and the lemon wedges in your pan and cook until the apples are soft. You may want to add a little water to prevent them from drying out too much – about 2 dessertspoons should be plenty. If you want to save time on washing up, cook them in an ovenproof/hobproof shal dish.

Remove the lemon wedges and throw these away. Stir in the sugar and cinnamon and remove from heat.

If you are not already using a shal ovenproof dish, transfer the apples into one now.

Cover the cooked apples with the honey-nut cornflakes. Dot the butter randomly among the cornflakes.

Place on the rack and turn the heat to 240°C (you are effectively grilling the top). Cook for 5–8 minutes until golden

Serve immediately with a dollop of crème fraîche or natural yoghurt.

Baked Honey and Ginger Pears

SERVES 2

1–2 pears, cored, peeled, and halved
Runny honey
¼ teaspoon mixed spice
4 ginger biscuits, crumbled
Vanilla ice-cream

Core, peel and halve your pears. Place them on a browning tray. Drizzle with a small amount of honey – try to keep this within the centre of the pears so it does not escape onto the tray as this may burn.

Set the temperature to 220°C and bake for 10–15 minutes.

While this is cooking you can crumble your ginger biscuits. Place them in a freezer bag and gently crush with a rolling pin.

Remove the pears from the oven, drizzle with more honey and a sprinkle of mixed spice. Cover with the crumbled ginger biscuits.

Place back in the oven and cook for another 5–10 minutes or until soft.

Serve with a generous dollop of vanilla ice-cream

Simple Hot Chocolate Soufflés

SERVES 2

Knob of softened butter
2 teaspoons caster sugar to line the ramekins
50g dark chocolate (at least 70% cocoa is the best)
2 eggs, separated
25g caster sugar, plus 1 teaspoon extra
Cocoa powder or icing sugar
Note: Serve with a dollop of crème fraîche for a delicious, indulgent pudding.

Rub the knob of butter around the inside of the ramekins to help prevent sticking. Sprinkle 2 teaspoons of caster sugar over the butter to form a layer. Shake off any residue sugar.

Melt the chocolate using a *bain marie* or a bowl over a pan of hot water, making sure the hot water does not touch the base of the bowl. Alternatively, you could melt the chocolate in a microwave.

While the chocolate is melting, mix the egg yolks with 25g of caster sugar until they become light and fluffy. Add the melted chocolate and combine well.

Whisk the egg whites until they form soft peaks. Add 1 teaspoon of sugar and whisk until thick.

Add a spoonful of the whisked egg white to the chocolate. Once combined, fold in the remaining egg white.

Preheat the NuWave Oven oven to HI.

Spoon the mixture into the ramekin dishes. Level the tops off.

Place on the rack and cook for 10 minutes, or until they are firm to the touch but slightly wobbly in the centre as you want them a bit gooey.

Remove from the oven and sprinkle with cocoa powder or icing sugar. Serve immediately in the ramekin dishes with a side dollop of crème fraîche.

www.ingramcontent.com/pod-product-compliance
Lightning Source LLC
Chambersburg PA
CBHW030943090426
42737CB00007B/524